NAUGHTY
NEWPORT

NAUGHTY NEWPORT

NOT TO MENTION
BALBOA ISLAND,
CORONA DEL MAR
AND MAYBE EVEN
LIDO ISLE

JUDGE ROBERT GARDNER

Newport Beach Historical Society Press
www.NewportBeachHistorical.com
E-mail: info@NewportBeachHistorical.com

ISBN: 978-0-615-85637-7
Library of Congress Control Number: 2013946281

This book was designed by Gordy Grundy
Proudly printed in the United States of America

CONTENTS

Forward

All families have stories, but not every family has a story teller. My father was certainly one. Like so many girls of my age, I grew up with Dorothy Gale and the Wizard of Oz, with Heidi in her Alps and Alice and her looking glass, but I also had all the stories that didn't come out of books but from my father. Because of his stories, Green River, Wyoming was just as vivid as the Emerald City as he told of a railroad strike there, his father's defiance of it, death threats, and how at the age of nine he was placed, by himself in the middle of the night, on a train which took him from Green River to Balboa. When I was older, the vixens of the cinema paled before his stories of my aunt who smuggled diamonds, was a shoe magnate's mistress in the Hollywood Hills, then a police chief's wife who adroitly explained the extra income the Feds were asking about. Everybody else's family seemed so boring in comparison. They weren't, of course. They just didn't have the proper narrative.

In addition to his narrative skills, my father had an eye for characters. We like and respect upright citizens, but we adore the rascals and villains, at least in literature, which explains the popularity of *Bawdy Balboa*. When talk of a sequel came up, he wasn't sure he had enough material, but he said he'd do it if I helped. I agreed, and we would sit at the breakfast bar in his house, throwing ideas back and forth. My mother would come in and ask what we were laughing about. "Well, you see," he would begin, "there was this guy. . ." And that's how *Naughty Newport* came about. There were these guys and there were these gals, and there was my father to tell their story.

Nancy Gardner
2013

Introduction

My name is Robert Gardner. Several years ago I penned a lighthearted romp through the history of the village of Balboa covering the period 1921 to 1941. In *Bawdy Balboa*, I tried to describe the honky-tonk flavor of Balboa during those years. Because of my rather myopic Balboa point of view, I'm afraid I gave the rest of the town a somewhat churlish back-of-the-hand treatment.

However, my Balboa era came to a screeching halt in 1942. That year I married and we had our first child–all in Balboa, of course. However, my wife, Katie, didn't share my love affair with Balboa. Actually, she couldn't stand the place. Somehow, and I've never been able to figure out how it was done, we moved from Balboa to Balboa Island, then to Corona del Mar, never to return to Balboa to live.

And now, some fifty years later, that first child, Nancy, who was born in Balboa but has no recollection of the place, either favorable or unfavorable, having left it before she was a year old, has suggested that the rest of the town deserves some of the same kind of treatment I gave Balboa. That seems fair. After all, there were some interesting people who did interesting things in other parts of the City of Newport Beach. And so I shall, with Nancy's help, endeavor to the best of my ability and recollection to paint a picture of the rest of the town.

As I said in *Bawdy Balboa*, others have written scholarly, comprehensive, accurate, precise and definitive histories of the City of Newport Beach. That which follows will be neither comprehensive, precise, definitive, scholarly nor necessarily accurate. Rather, it will be an effort to portray the flavor of the town, "warts, wrinkles and all," to quote Oliver Cromwell's advice to the painter doing his portrait.

Robert Gardner
1999

NAUGHTY NEWPORT

NOT TO MENTION

BALBOA ISLAND,
CORONA DEL MAR

AND MAYBE EVEN

LIDO ISLE

NEWPORT

Book One

NEWPORT

From the time the McFadden brothers built their wharf, the area now known as Old Newport was a vibrant, bustling community. Balboa was a couple of shacks at a place called Abbott's Landing, Balboa Island was a mud flat and Corona del Mar a place where Mr. Irvine grazed his cattle, but Newport actually had an economy. Balboa eventually caught on, but even then it was simply a honky-tonk summer resort that existed on liquor, gambling, a couple of dance halls and hamburgers–lots of hamburgers. During the winter, it went into hibernation. Newport, on the other hand, was commercial–with a commercial fishing fleet, a commercial wharf, a commercial railroad and a stable year-round population.

That doesn't mean nothing ever happened there.

Stark's Saloon

The next time the Newport Beach Historical Society feels a compulsion to install one of those bronze historical markers, I suggest it give serious consideration to Stark's Saloon. Given the personality of our town, historical recognition of a pioneer saloon would not seem inappropriate. It would appear to be at least as appropriate as the plaque honoring Glenn Martin's hydroplane flight from Balboa Bay to Avalon and back in 1912. While that was a memorable event, to me the most newsworthy aspect of Mr. Martin's feat was the speech made by the German mayor of Santa Ana honoring Mr. Martin because he had "flown der vater offer chust like a lion."

Henry Stark opened his saloon in 1902 on that funny little half-block street in Newport called 21st Place. The site was later occupied by Sid's Blue Beet.

It may seem odd that a saloon was opened in 1902 when the city was not even incorporated until 1906. However, it must be remembered that McFadden's Wharf was erected in 1899, and by 1902 Newport was practically a bustling metropolis complete with a commercial wharf and a railway to Santa Ana, not to mention the beginnings of a fishing fleet. Given that many thirsty men (women were not allowed in saloons), it is not surprising that Newport had a saloon.

During Prohibition, Stark's lost its identity as a saloon. Nevertheless, the place remained open as a cafe, and I am advised that Henry Stark treated Prohibition with the same lofty disdain as did Balboa with its justly famous Drugless Drugstore where you couldn't buy as much as an aspirin tablet, but straight alcohol was for sale across the counter at two bits an ounce.

However, before, during and after Prohibition, Stark's boasted several items of historical interest. The first was the longest-running poker game in Newport Beach or probably anywhere else. Separated from the bar by a thin wall, that poker game went on for twenty-four hours at a stretch. When the bar closed at two, to reopen at six, the poker players just closed the door between the bar and the room housing the poker game and kept playing. Not being a poker player, I never got into the game, but I used to glance into that room from time to time and could recognize fishermen, cannery workers and local business and professional men. It was a town institution. It started shortly after Henry Stark opened the place in 1902 and ran until the Stark family sold the place to Sid Sauffer in 1960. That's a long time for any game to run.

Another item of historical interest at Stark's was its back bar–a real, authentic Western mining town back bar. It was said that Henry Stark purchased the back bar in Cripple Creek and somehow transported it to Newport Beach. Whether that back bar came from Cripple Creek or not, it compared favorably with any back bar seen today in such tourist traps as Virginia City or Leadville, with a great mirror surrounded by all kinds of carved wood. All it needed was a painting of either a naked woman or Custer's Last Stand for pure authenticity.

That back bar had its ups and downs. In 1960 when Sid Sauffer bought the place, he kept the back bar as part of his Blue Beet operation. When the Blue Beet burned down, the back bar was damaged. Not to worry. Sid simply moved it to his new restaurant located at Whiskey Bill's old place on Newport Boulevard. There he was engaged in refurbishing the back bar when he ran into trouble with the City of Costa Mesa about too many old cars in his front yard, and the refurbishing job was put on what turned out to be a permanent hold.

Another item of historical interest concerning Stark's was its price list. For fifteen cents you could get a straight shot with either a beer, Coke or ginger ale chaser. Obviously, for a buck you could buy drinks for the house. An added fillip was that the bartender bought every third drink. At least he did when Al Horvath, Bert Oquist or Shorte Charle were the bartenders. It's real hard to find drinks in that price range today.

Another item that deserves mention in any in-depth historical discussion is the old gal they called Dollar Dolly.

I first met Dollar Dolly in 1936 when I was working nights as a policeman during that awful first starvation year of law practice in Balboa. My shift was from four pm until midnight, and invariably after my shift I went to Stark's for a snack. There I met Dolly, a raddled old broad who trolled for customers at Stark's and the Stag. I have no idea how old Dolly was, but she was no spring chicken. She had shiny dyed-black hair and pancake makeup so thick it looked as though it was made from real pancake dough. Two red-rimmed eyes peered out at the world from about a pound of mascara. I don't know how she ever got a customer, but I know they must have been hard up. I have no idea when Dolly began her career. Everyone I asked said she had been around as long as they could remember.

I won't go so far as to suggest that there should be a bronze plaque erected honoring Dollar Dolly as an historical monument, but I do think she merits some recognition as an institution in Old Newport.

Charbonneau L H (Orange) 1223 W Bay av Newport
Charle Don (Betty) asst mgr Arches Serv Station r 4102
    River av Newport
Charle Lionel (Winifred) serv sta attdt r 125½ Apolena
    av Balboa Island
Charlebois E Lionel Lily) mgr Warren Craft r Bay
    Shores—162
Chase Blanche Mrs r 120 23d st Newport
Chatain R L (LA) 118 Ruby av Balboa Island
Chatterton Frank C h 114 27th st Newport
Cheek Ida Ann Mrs (Pasadena) 910 E Surf Balboa
Cherry David (Lucy) tchr Grammar Schl r 1520 Ocean
    Fr Newport
Cherry D H Mrs r 1520 Ocean Fr Newport
Cheesman C D (LA) 1126 E Central av Balboa
Chew Randall T Jr (Covina) 3912 Channel pl Nwpt Isl
Childs B F slsmn r 210 Abalone av Balboa Island
Childs Clyde (Edith) painter r 114 E Bay av Balboa
Childs Herman (Mary) r 828 W Surf Balboa

CHRIS-CRAFT SALES & SERVICE (McKenzie Corpn)
    925 State Highway Newport—894

Christ Church-by-the-Sea (Wm R Hessell pastor) W Cen-
    tral & 14th st Newport
Christensen A E (Anaheim) 715 W Central av Balboa
Christensen C E Mrs r 206 Apolena av Balboa Island
Christensen Louis P (LA) 218 Sapphire av Balboa Island
Christian Science Reading Room (Mrs Julia R Dickinson
    librarian 118 E Central av Balboa
City Camp Grounds (Wm Ulrich mgr) 18th st & Bay Fr
    Newport

Shorte Charle

As I said, I began to go to Stark's when I was a policeman. Then, after I became the city judge, I continued eating my lunch there. It was very convenient, just across McFadden Square from the Police Department and City Hall. Our prisoners all ate their lunches there, so when I went to lunch I could look forward to some interesting conversations with those I had just sentenced to jail.

One day I was having lunch at Stark's and talking to the bartender, Shorte Charle. A big, beefy man down the bar, not one of the prisoners, began to give me a bad time about some case I had tried in which he had been involved. Before I had time to even look at the guy Shorte jumped over the bar and knocked him off his bar stool. The guy landed on his rump, shook his head to clear it, put his hands down on either side for support, leaned back, looked up at Shorte and said, "Why the hell did you do that, Shorte?"

Shorte replied, "Because the judge is an old friend of mine."

Shorte Charle was indeed an old friend. He and I had worked together when the Rendezvous Ballroom opened in 1928.

Originally, the Rendezvous opened as a nickel-a-dance place. Shorte and I were gate boys. That meant we stood at little gates and collected tickets from the dancers as they entered the dance floor. After each dance we took long ropes out onto the dance floor and herded or dragged the dancers off. Obviously, the Rendezvous was a class operation.

After a couple of years as gate boys, Shorte and I quit the Rendezvous. I stayed in Balboa and began working as a counterman and waiter at the Green Dragon. Shorte drifted up the peninsula to Newport. He was a drinking man and soon made Stark's his headquarters, and with that as a background graduated to the job of bartender.

Shorte was also a fighter. Being a drinking man and a fighter was an unfortunate combination, given Shorte's size–about five foot six and one hundred forty pounds wringing wet. As a result, Shorte lost all his front teeth rather early on. I never asked how he lost them, but I can imagine it happened in much the same way my law school buddy Greg Bautzer lost his.

Greg, who later became a prominent lawyer in the entertainment world, came to Balboa with me one weekend. In the Rendezvous, he became involved in one of those silly shoving matches with an oil field worker from Huntington Beach. They agreed to go out on the beach and settle the matter. Greg was taking off his jacket and had it just around his elbows when the oil field worker let him have a haymaker to the mouth, breaking all Greg's front teeth. Greg had his replaced. Shorte never did.

Shorte had another talent besides drinking and fighting. He was a swimmer. In those days there was a yearly swim from the Newport pier to the Balboa pier. Every year Shorte would sober up long enough to enter the race, and he always won. This was a matter of some frustration to the more athletically inclined swimmers who had actually trained for the event. Shorte's only training was at Stark's and the Stag.

However, the most historically memorable event in Shorte's Newport career was the great manhole caper.

A manhole cover (I suppose that today in our effort to neuterize our language we call them peoplehole covers) is a very heavy iron object, about three or four feet in diameter and about three inches thick. It must weigh several hundred pounds and be very awkward to carry.

One night someone (or someones) took a manhole cover off the street about six blocks from the place where Shorte lived. Officer Jack Kennedy of the Newport Beach Police Department found the manhole cover in Shorte's room, right beside his bed. When awakened, Shorte denied any knowledge of it. Nevertheless, Officer Kennedy arrested Shorte for theft of the manhole cover.

The trial was old home week for Rendezvous Ballroom alumni as all three of us–Shorte, Jack Kennedy and I–had worked together at the Rendezvous during its nickel-a-dance era.

The prosecution was simple and straightforward. Someone had taken the manhole cover, the property of the City of Newport Beach, and transported it six blocks to the place where Shorte had a room. There the manhole cover had been transported up a flight of stairs where it was found in Shorte's room with Shorte asleep beside it. A circumstantial case, it was true, but strong circumstances, possession of stolen property and all that jazz.

The defense was equally straightforward. Shorte went to bed one night with no manhole cover in his room. When he awoke there was the manhole cover on the floor beside his bed plus his old friend, Officer Jack Kennedy. That was all he knew.

I found Shorte not guilty. I had several reasons for my decision. First, although Shorte was a boozer and a fighter, he was no thief. Neither was he a liar. Additionally, there was no way that Shorte, drunk or sober, could have gotten that manhole cover from its normal resting place six blocks down

Central Avenue, then up a flight of stairs to his room. Additionally, the theft aspect of the case fell flat. There is very little commercial activity in the used manhole market. If he had stolen it, the only buyer would have been the City of Newport Beach–and not even the dumbest thief would have tried to sell the city's manhole cover back to the city.

The whole thing smelled of a prank. This was reinforced by a rumor around Stark's that Jiggs Dyson and Rebel Brown had pulled the whole thing as a joke on Shorte. Knowing Jiggs and Rebel, this made a lot of sense.

Jiggs Dyson and Rebel Brown

Jiggs Dyson and Rebel Brown were commercial fishermen. They were also drinking men, fighting men and all-around hell-raisers. I should point out that when I refer to someone as a drinking man, I mean no disrespect. Those who grew up during Prohibition were, generally speaking, drinking people. That which was prohibited became a challenge. Actually, the only person whom I can say with any degree of certainty was not a drinking person was Flora Beatty who lived on Anade Street in Balboa. The reason I knew Mrs. Beatty didn't drink was because one summer I was a postman and delivered to her the WCTU (Women's Christian Temperance Union) magazine. She had the only subscription in town and was the only one to wear the white ribbon signifying membership in the organization.

Prohibition was an unmitigated disaster. Not only did it ruin the drinking habits of a generation of Americans, it destroyed a generation of American law enforcement officers who simply gave up trying to enforce an unenforceable law. It also laid the foundation for the big city gangs which exist to this day. But enough of moralizing.

Jiggs and Rebel were natural suspects in the Shorte Charle manhole cover incident. It was the sort of crazy thing Jiggs and Rebel would think of.

Pull a manhole cover off the street, roll it six blocks, lug it up a flight of stairs and plant it in Shorte's room, then back to Stark's to imagine the look on Shorte's face when he woke up to find a manhole cover in his room.

I liked Jiggs and Rebel. Pranks like the Shorte Charle/manhole cover caper were funny to me. However, my affection for the two of them was strained one night at the Army-Navy Club in Long Beach.

I don't know why it was called the Army-Navy Club because it was open to anyone. It was located on Ocean Boulevard near its intersection with Cherry Avenue. It was a converted mansion on the bluff facing the ocean. One entered at street level, then descended down some very impressive sweeping stairs to the dining room. It was quite a place.

And so it was that when I was wooing Katie, my future wife, I took her one night to the Army-Navy Club to impress her. I was being smooth, clever, debonair, fascinating–the whole schmeer.

Suddenly, there was a commotion at the head of the stairs. I looked up, and to my horror, there were Jiggs Dyson and Rebel Brown fighting with all the restaurant help who were trying to keep them out of the place–five or six men trying to keep the two of them out, but those were cinch odds for Jiggs and Rebel. They were throwing restaurant help all over the place. Then Jiggs happened to look down the stairs to the dining room. I tried to hide, but it was too late.

Jiggs roared, "Reb, that's the judge down there!"

They plunged down the steps, knocking resistance out of the way like bowling pins. Rebel was particularly effective since he'd broken his arm in a fight a few days before, and his arm was in a cast. He used the cast very effectively.

They tossed off the last of the restaurant people, gathered a couple of chairs from nearby tables, dumping on the floor those who had been using the chairs, pulled the chairs up and sat down exuding whiskey fumes and friendship.

They stayed about a half hour, the longest half hour of my life, telling the woman I was trying to impress outlandish, ribald stories about me and making clear that I was their favorite judge because I shared the same moral standards they possessed.

They finally left and, wonder of wonders, my future wife was neither sad nor shocked. Instead, she was almost hysterical with laughter. She said that up until then she had thought I was kind of stuffy, but if I had friends like that I couldn't be all bad.

Dyson Geo (Pearl) boat oper r 119 29th st Newport
Dyson Nellie real est brkr ofc 2700 Ocean Fr Newport
Dyson Walter E ptlmn r 418 Santa Ana av Newport Hts

— E —

Eadington T (Fullerton) 1710 Ocean Fr Newport
Eagan Geo (So Pasa) 213 Topaz av Balboa Island
Eames Milo D (LA) 106 Grand Canal Balboa Island
Earel F E Dr (Santa Ana) 227 Grand Canal Balboa Isl
Earl's Landing (Earl R Tibbits) 1215 State Highway
Earnshaw Fenton W r 1600 E Central av Balboa
Earnshaw Harry A (Vena) h 1600 E Central av Balboa
Earnshaw Harry Lewis r 1600 E Central av Balboa
East Newport Market (Carl A Danielson—J F Watkins
    508 W Central av Balboa—115
Eastman Burns Dr h 206 Coral av Balboa Island
Eastman Frederic W (Emma) h 134 Via Yella Lido Isle
Eastman Ruth Gilbert (Brea) 124 Topaz av Balboa Isl
Eastman Oscar (Mae) fshmn r 211 21st st Newport
Eastman Spalding clk South Coast Marine Supply r 134
    Via Yella Lido Isle
Eastman Wm (Lillian) fshmn r 211 21st st Newport
Eastvedt Carl (Helen) photo Hitchcock r 205 7th Balboa
Ebell Club 515 W Central av Balboa
Eckert M V Mrs mgr Beach House r 516 W Ceneral Bal
Eckley Susan Mrs h 1316 E Central av Balboa
Economy Serv Station (Balaton & Kitchen) 6504 St Hiwy
Eddy Al boatmn r 1628 Ocean Fr Newport
Eddy Ella Mrs r 209 E Bay Fr Balboa Island
Eddy Myron Fish (Eliz) r 209 E Bay Fr Balboa Island
Eden Lester (Ruth) Eden's Garage r 207 Agate Bal Isl
Eden's Garage (Lester Eden) 122 Agate av Bal Isl—520
Edgar Mildred L (Pasa) 907 N Bay Fr Balboa Island
Edgar Oceana V (Santa Ana) 416 E Bay av Balboa
Edge E R (San Brndno) 413 Fernleaf av Corona del Mar
Edgewater Tavern 501 Edgewater pl Balboa
Edick C H (Hungtn Pk) 116 38th st Newport
Edison Co of So Calif (J D Watkins local agt) 712 E
    Central av Balboa—54

The Dory Fisherman

Walt Dyson, brother of Jiggs Dyson, was one of the most powerful men I have ever known. That was because he had been a dory fisherman.

In the early days of dory fishing, the fishermen rowed their dories through the surf, then several miles out into the ocean, there to do their fishing. In so doing, they became immensely strong, especially in the arms and shoulders.

They rowed for the simple reason that mankind had not as yet invented a retractable propeller for boats. If you came into the beach with a propeller-driven craft, as soon as you hit the sand you lost your propeller.

An ingenious local dory fisherman named Shorty Guenther thought he had the answer. Shorty equipped his boat with an airplane engine on a stand, attached a propeller to it and, voila, he was off to the fishing grounds without having to row a stroke. It was a grand idea. Shorty started out just fine. The engine made a lot of noise, the propeller whirled, the boat entered the water. The first wave hit the boat, the boat stopped, but the airplane engine, propeller and Shorty didn't. They just kept going. That was the end of Shorty Guenther's bid for immortality in dory fishing history. Dory fishermen continued to row and continued to be very powerful men.

When I first met Walt Dyson he was a member of the Newport Beach Police Department, a big, slow-moving, unflappable man who fit right in with George Callihan, Frank Naylor and Kenny Gorton in handling the noisy, boisterous, often unruly crowds on Main Street in Balboa on Saturday nights.

If someone became too boisterous, Walt just lifted him up gently by the front of his clothes, shook him a couple of times while his feet dangled, then, upon the man's promise to behave himself, put him down. It was very effective, more effect than mace, stun guns or pepper spray.

Jack Gillis, another dory fisherman, had the same concept in quelling prospective trouble. I was at a party at his house one night when Shorte Charle got out of line. Jack grabbed Shorte by the front of his clothes, shook him a couple of times, put him down, and Shorte was the best-behaved man at the party after that.

Jack had a son, Johnny, who was a very special friend of mine. From his youth as a dory fisherman, Johnny was also very powerful. That strength resulted in a somewhat bothersome social practice insofar as his old–and skinny–friend Bob Gardner was concerned. At parties, Johnny had the habit of putting his arm around me, then forgetting he had done so. He would walk around with me tucked snugly under his arm, my feet dragging, until I could squeal enough to get his attention at which time he would apologize for this thoughtlessness and let me go. Dory fishermen were strong.

Bob Reed

Another strong man was Bob Reed. However, Bob didn't acquire his strength rowing a dory several miles a day in the open sea. Bob was an iceman. He acquired his strength wrestling three-hundred-pound slabs of ice.

I know that everyone under seventy years of age will have trouble believing it, but at one stage in society's climb up the ladder of civilization, there were no ice cubes. Really. I kid you not.

Ice came not in handy cubes but in huge slabs about five feet long, five inches thick, three or four feet wide. Each slab weighed about three hundred pounds. Also, believe it or not, there were no refrigerators. Instead, there were iceboxes on the top of which there were lids which, when lifted, led to a container into which blocks of ice were placed. That ice came via an iceman who drove up in a truck loaded with those huge three-hundred-pound slabs. He would chip off a slab that would fit into a particular icebox and put that slab into the icebox. The icebox was usually kept on the back porch. There was a good reason for that placement. As the ice melted in the box it dripped into a tray which had to be emptied regularly. If one forgot to empty the tray, it overflowed. Thus, the icebox was kept on the back porch to minimize dam-

29

age. Yankee ingenuity.

Because I grew up during the pre-cube portion of our ice age, my first job, at the age of ten, was that of an ice chipper. When a restaurant bought a slab of ice, someone had to chop that slab into small enough pieces to fit into a glass. I was that someone at the Green Dragon Cafe in Balboa. I had two ice picks, one the typical single prong. With that one I cut off enough ice to fit into the ice container behind the counter. The other ice pick had a series of parallel prongs. This one was used to cut the ice so that it would fit into a glass.

The ice chipper was pretty far down the social scale in a restaurant, just one jump ahead of the dishwasher who was usually a drunk and who was, in turn, about one jump ahead of a sideshow geek, the guy who bit heads off chickens. The ice chipper was pretty far down the wage scale, also. I was paid ten cents an hour.

Because of my contact with ice, I stood in awe of icemen. They were strong. They had to be to wrestle those ungainly three-hundred-pound slabs of ice around. Bob Reed was our iceman.

Bob was the son of Clarence Reed, owner and operator of the Newport Ice Company located on 30th Street in old Newport. I never saw Clarence Reed touch a piece of ice unless it was in a cocktail glass. Handling the ice slabs was Bob's job.

And so I had the good fortune to see the great iceman race in Balboa sometime during the late twenties. Bob Reed and a man from the Santa Ana Ice Company were the contestants. The race was around the block and started in front of the Green Dragon. Each of the contestants was attired in the traditional iceman's costume, a long leather cape that hung down the back to keep water from the melting ice on his back from saturating the iceman's clothes.

Two identical, carefully weighed three-hundred-pound slabs of ice were placed on the sidewalk. On the count of three, each iceman grabbed his ice tongs, jammed them into his block of ice, hoisted the block of ice onto his back and took off down Main Street toward the pier. At the boardwalk they turned to the right past Dirty George's hamburger joint and the bathhouse, then to the right on Washington to Central, then right again past the old Rendezvous located where the Balboa Theater now sits vacant, and to the finish line back at the Green Dragon. The two icemen came charging down the sidewalk neck and neck. The judges declared Bob the winner by an ice pick. It was a thrilling race.

My next exposure to Bob Reed was somewhat more traumatic. Tagg Atwood and I, as a couple of normally obnoxious beach urchins, had developed a practice by which we stood at the water's edge and ostensibly threw wet sand at each other. Of course, somehow we kept missing each other and pelting unwary tourists with wet sand. It was great fun.

One day this big, blond smiling man came walking down toward the water. Tagg and I stood there casually throwing wet sand at each other and measuring just the right time to pelt this unsuspecting fellow when he reached the water's edge. When he came within range we just happened to miss each other and pelted him with globs of sand. The big, blond, smiling man didn't say a word. He just grabbed each of us by the back of the neck and marched us out into the surf where he held our heads under water until we thought we were going to drown. After I finished throwing up salt water I recognized the big, blond, smiling man. It was Bod Reed the iceman. I hadn't known him without his iceman costume. Tagg and I quit throwing wet sand at tourists after that.

Bob Reed was not only a man of immense strength. He was also an astute businessman. He had several successful businesses, culminating in the purchase and operation of Charlie TeWinkle's hardware store in Costa Mesa which he operated for several years. Sharp businessman though he was, however, one of his more memorable business ventures was a disaster. That was the great whale fiasco.

One year a great big dead whale washed up on the beach next to the Newport pier. Bob Reed saw the commercial opportunity it offered. He secured permission from the city council, rented a circus tent, put the tent over the whale and charged admission. At first it was a great success. People stood in line to see and touch this great monster of the deep. However, a problem soon arose. After a few days in the hot sun under that circus tent, the whale began to decompose. I guess that everything that decomposes begins to smell. However, dead fish are in a class by themselves. It was for that reason that John Randolph of Roanoke chose a dead fish when he uttered his famous phrase to the effect that his political enemies "shine and stink like rotten mackerel in the moonlight." A few tons of dead whale stink a lot worse than a single dead mackerel.

Bob took down his circus tent, but that wasn't enough. All the merchants along the oceanfront began to complain. So did the homeowners up and down the beach. The city council ordered Bob to remove the carcass. Bob hired a tug to pull the whale off the beach and into the water, but the whale came to pieces and couldn't be towed. It was too big to bury. Whale blubber never had much of a market except among Eskimos. So Bob finally had to cut the stinking monster into truck-size pieces and haul them away.

Just where he disposed of those truck-size pieced he never said.

The Okie Fishing Fleet

In the early days there were four fishing fleets in Southern California. Three were made up of distinct ethnic groups. There was the Portuguese fishing fleet in San Diego. There was the Yugoslav fishing fleet in San Pedro. There was the Japanese fishing fleet in Fish Harbor on Terminal Island. And there was the Newport Beach fishing fleet, a polyglot group without any distinctive ethnic identity. It's a little hard to identify as an ethnic group fishermen with names such as McMillen, Hales, Shafer, Mills, Dyson, Dixon, Johnson, Sharps and Anich. Finally, my oldest friend, Marco Anich, son of pioneer fisherman Pete Anich, came up with a name for the Newport group–the Okie Fishing Fleet.

Newport Beach had a fishing fleet from the very beginning, an integral part of the local economy. As a Balboan, I was only vaguely aware of it and then only because in the early hours of the morning we could hear the Newport fishermen going to work. In those days, before the harbor was dredged, what is now Newport Harbor was a maze of mud flats, sand bars, sand islands and swamps. A narrow channel ran from the Rhine where the fishing fleet made its home to the Newport Harbor Yacht Club, hugging the bay side of the peninsula. At the yacht club, it turned left around Bay Island, then went between mud flats to a channel Joe Beek had dredged through the Bay Island mud flat so his ferry could cross. The fishermen then followed a narrow channel next to the peninsula up to the point where the always hazardous harbor mouth awaited. Beyond that was the ocean and fish.

Then came the Great Depression, and the so-called Okies began to escape the Dust Bowl by coming to California. Most of them went to the Central Valley and were immortalized by John Steinbeck in *The Grapes of Wrath*. Some didn't get as far as Fresno. Some only got as far as Newport Beach. There, dirt farmers though they were, they became fishermen. Of course, they didn't know diddly about fishing. For example, about this time scoop fishing for mackerel became popular. The traditional way of fishing for mackerel was with jigs. However, someone discovered that by holding a light over the water at night, the curious mackerel would come up to look at the light, and you could simply scoop them aboard. The Okies were thrilled at this easier way to catch fish, so thrilled that a good many of them scooped up so many mackerel aboard they swamped their boats. Hence, the Okie fishing fleet.

Unfortunately, all these fishermen plus the live bait boats plus sport fishing from every yacht in the harbor finally caught all the fish in the Catalina channel. The canneries closed and our Okie fishing fleet disappeared.

Horse Fisherman

The first year I came to Balboa, 1921, I attended the old grammar school at 14th Street and the oceanfront. (That building was condemned after the 1931 Long Beach earthquake.) I think I was in the fourth grade. Following my rather nomadic father around from railroad town to railroad town, the various schools I went to and the grades attended are something of a blur. However, that year at the Newport Beach Grammar School is etched in my memory.

From time to time, men and horses pulled fish up on the beach in front of the school. I was pretty much in the dark about how this happened until Marco Anich straightened me out. Marco was the son of a Dalmatian fisherman named Pete Anich. Pete was a fine man, very much of a leader among the fishermen and, through Marco, a friend of mine. Pete always called me Booby. I contend that this was because he spoke with a Dalmatian accent. Marco denies this. He says his father called me Booby because he meant booby.

Be that as it may, it is through Marco that I finally learned the true facts about fishermen and the horses that dragged fish up on the beach in front of the old Newport Beach Grammar School.

According to Marco, the fish I saw being pulled up on the beach were jacksmelt. During the jacksmelt season, the local fishermen kept a man stationed at the end of the Newport pier. His job was to spot schools of jacksmelt. These schools appear as large, dark underwater clouds just outside the breaker line. Once spotted, and not necessarily in front of the grammar school, a dory and a big net were hauled to that spot. There the fishermen in the dory dragged the net through the breakers and around the school of fish. Then a team of horses pulled the net, together with all those fish, up on the beach.

Marco's memory of this is particularly acute because his father owned the horses and Marco had the honor of riding the horses to the location where the fish had been spotted.

When the fish were pulled in, the fishermen scooped them up, they were placed in a truck and then hauled to the fish markets of John Horman or Frank Suttora. There they were washed, put into boxes, covered with ice and hauled to Los Angeles on the Pacific Electric. The Newport kids were paid for washing and packing the fish. We Balboans were never invited to take part in that aspect of the operation. The only thing we Balboans were allowed to do was to become victims in the great jellyfish wars.

Invariably, when the fishing operation was taking place, school let out. We Balboans, happy in our ignorance, thought it was so we could help bring in the fish and ran down to the water's edge where we tried to catch the slippery smelt with our bare hands, an exercise in futility. The Newport kids knew better. They ignored the smelt and grabbed the jellyfish that came in with them, pelting us until we were covered with the things, laughing as we ran home yelling from the stings.

The Saga of Deefy Johnson

I have mentioned the poker game in the back room of Stark's. It was a well-policed game. One night the players caught a guy cheating and threw him out of the game. He was a stranger in town. He was also drunk and mean. However, rather than take his pique out on the poker players, he decided to terrorize the patrons in the bar. He pulled a knife with a six-inch blade and charged into the bar swinging the knife.

The first man he came to was Big Bill Ponting, our local constable, who was leaning back on the bar, cowboy hat on his head, red face exuding friendship for all, his rather prominent belly protruding. The stranger took a swipe at Bill with his knife, Bill pulled in his considerable paunch and let the knife slide harmlessly by, then admonished the knife wielder to be careful or he might hurt someone. Bill took a tolerant view of activities other law enforcement officers might deem antisocial.

The stranger went through the crowd, slashing away at people who just dodged out of the way and went on with their normal activities. It took quite a bit to disturb the crowd at Stark's. After all, they were used to Jiggs Dyson and Rebel Brown.

Finally, the knife wielder came to Deefy Johnson. I never did know

Deefy's first name. Deefy was stone deaf, allegedly because he tried to light a cigarette one morning when he tried to start his fishing boat. You are supposed to air out the bilges. Deefy didn't, the boat blew up and Deefy's ears blew in. Whether the story was true or not, Deefy was deaf.

Deefy was sitting there in a rocking chair, minding his own business. Just why there was a rocking chair in a bar I have no idea, but Stark's was like that–original. Anyway, Deefy was just sitting there rocking away, minding his own business in his own quiet world. The knife wielder took a slash at Deefy who took a dim view of anyone who interrupted his silent musings.

Deefy stood up, picked up the chair, broke it into several pieces, grabbed a rocker and took off after the knife wielder. Deefy chased the guy all around McFadden Square, swinging the rocker every time he got close. Some busybody called the police, and George Callihan responded to the call. Actually, the phone panel in the police department lighted up like the Tournament of Lights as people called in from Suttora's Fish Market, Horman's Fish Market, Cottle's Grocery Store and the Newport Theater, as people in those places saw Deefy going by swinging away with his rocker at the guy with the knife. When Callihan arrived, the chase had returned to McFadden Square. Over the parked cars, Cal could see Deefy swinging away at something. Cal began to thread his way through the parked cars to get close enough to Deefy to find out what or who Deefy was swinging at. Just then Deefy caught up with the knife wielder and decked him with a roundhouse swing of the rocker. Deefy had gotten him dead center, splitting his scalp very neatly. Callihan took the guy to Doc Grundy who spent the rest of the night stitching the guy's head together.

The next morning, the knife wielder appeared in my court with so many bandages it looked like he was wearing a turban. He paid the usual fifty dollar fine for disturbing the peace. Then he asked Chief of Police Rowland Hodgkinson what was being done about the guy who almost killed him.

"Nothing," said Hodge.

"What do you mean, nothing? The guy almost killed me!"

"He was acting in self-defense," Hodge said.

"Self-defense?" the guy screamed. "He chased me for blocks."

"Self-defense, Newport Beach style," smiled Hodge.

And so a new legal concept was born–self-defense, Newport Beach style. Geographic self-defense.

Holman Kathryn r 133 Turquoise av Balboa Island
Holmberg Edwin (Ethel) pattern mkr h 411 Fernleaf C D M
Holmes C F (Colton) 116 25th st Newport
Holmes Mark (LA) 5804 Ocean Fr Newport
Holtz Harold R (Lucille) h 306 Apolena av Balboa Island
Homer Harry (So Pasa) 3700 Coast blvd Newport
Homeyer Harry r Bay Shore Camp
Honeycutt Walter (Clara) firemn r 537 S A av Npt Hts
Honeyman Robt B Jr (San Marina) 2009 E Bay Fr Balboa
Hood Hubert E elec Grill r 306 Fernando st Balboa
Hood J H Mrs (Pasa) 212 Ruby av Balboa Island
Hood Minnie Mrs r 308 Fernando st Balboa
Hook Mabel E h 108 7th st Balboa
Hook Rufus M (Perris) 104 Island av Balboa
Hooker C W (Bev Hills) 409 N Bay Fr Balboa Island
Hooper Jess (Aytrelle) oilwkr r 1910 Court av Newport
Hopkins C Harold (Louise) h 1707 E Bay Fr Balboa—716
Hooping Anna S (Pasadena) 7002 Ocean Fr Newport
Hormen J P retail fish mkt 110 McFadden pl Newport
Hormen J P wholesale fish dealr 2320 W Central av New-
    port—350-W, r same
Horn Frank N (Mabel) h 211 Agate av Balboa Island
Horner Geo W (Helen) r 113 15th st Newport
Horner Geo W J r 113 15th st Newport
Horner Mary Miss r 113 15th st Newport
Horrell C H (Dorothy) yd formn Hayward Lbr r 129 25th
    st Newport
Horvath Frank fshmn r 2822 W Central av Newport

John Horman

John Horman was a fixture in early Newport. He operated a fish dock on the bayfront at the location now occupied by Woody's Wharf. From that dock John bought fresh fish from the local commercial fishermen for resale in Los Angeles. He lived there on the deck together with lots of pigeons and even more fish. Understandably, he always smelled of fish. He was rather small, had a lined face, scraggly mustache and always wore a grungy, shiny blue serge suit.

I first met John Horman when I was rather small. Charley Plummer, who taught me almost everything worthwhile I ever learned, had taught me how to catch octopus on the mud flats and how to sell them to Mr. Horman. And so it was that from time to time I would trudge up from Balboa to Newport carrying a pail of octopus to sell to John Horman. However, the money was strictly a secondary reason for the trip. The real reason was to watch Mr. Horman bite an octopus.

Biting an octopus to death is considered a kind of rite of manhood around the Mediterranean Sea and on certain Pacific islands. It seems there is a nerve that runs between the eyes of an octopus. If severed, the octopus dies. A long time ago, some show-off on some Pacific island or Mediterranean shorefront bit an octopus between the eyes, cut the nerve and caused the octopus to die. It became the macho thing to do. John Horman carried on the tradition.

Knowing what I came for, he would reach into my bucket, haul out a good-sized octopus and hold it up to his face. The octopus would assume the traditional octopus fighting stance with all tentacles laid back. John would pull the octopus right up to his face. The tentacles of the octopus would wrap around John's head and face. John would start snapping away, and while he was snapping, the octopus would be squirting its ink. The purple ink would drip off John's mustache and chin, the tentacles would writhe, and then suddenly John would find his mark. All eight of the tentacles would collapse, and John would emerge triumphant. It was a very thrilling sight to watch. With that as a background, it's not surprising I remember John Horman so favorably.

At one time, John was a drinking man. If he wasn't at his fish dock, he could be found at Stark's or the Stag. Then one day when he was in his cups he drove his ancient Model-T roadster, converted to a pickup, down Central Avenue at its top speed of about fifteen to twenty miles an hour. In the 800 block he lost control of the vehicle and ran it up on the sidewalk. Unfortunately, there were on that same sidewalk three teenagers on their way to the Ritz Theater in Balboa. He ran over all three, inflicting on them painful but not serious injuries. John was hauled off to the city jail and the youngsters taken to Dr. Gordon Grundy's small hospital at 9th and Central which was only a block from the accident scene.

There Dr. Grundy began to treat the young people for their assorted cuts, bruises and abrasions. When he saw the kids weren't seriously hurt, he called Chief of Police Rowland Hodgkinson and told him to bring John from the jail so he could witness the painful medical treatment the young people were going through. Hodge complied, and John sat through three hours of watching the medical procedures. Hodge always claimed that Dr. Grundy encouraged the young people to whoop and holler during their treatment. True or not, from that moment on John Horman never took another drink. As a matter of fact, the experience was so painful for John that he never drove a car again. If we had Gordon Grundy and Rowland Hodgkinson working as a team today, we could cut down on drinking and driving to a considerable extent.

John Horman was very fond of me for a minor favor I had done for him when I was in private practice before I became a judge. Thus every Christmas I would get a call from John. In a voice that could best be described as a high-pitched, breathless, heavily-accented whine, he would say, "Jawdge, this is John. You come over. I got something for you." When I arrived at his dock he would give me a big bull lobster.

It was during one of those yearly visits that John asked me if it was necessary that everyone have a will. I said it wasn't. He asked what would happen if someone died and didn't leave a will. I said that by operation of law his estate would go to his heirs. He asked what would happen if someone didn't have any heirs. I said that his estate would go to the State of California through a process known as escheat. John's face lit up. "I like that," he said. "That's what I want." He explained that he came from Russia and had left because the Russian Revolution was in full swing and there was no government. When he came to California, the government allowed him to go into business and make money, and for that he was very appreciative. He said he wanted his property to go to the State because without the State he would have nothing.

I asked him if he was sure he had no heirs, no remote relatives. He said he had no one in either category. I said that just in case he was mistaken, he should draw up a will and leave his property to the State if that was what he wanted. I also suggested that he might want to remember Casper, his driver and dock assistant. John shook his head. I got the same response when I suggested he might want to remember Hannah Gillis who had run his fresh fish shop by the police department for many years. John was adamant. He wanted all his property to go to the State of California.

A few years later John died, and to the surprise of many of us, he left quite an estate. It seems that during the Depression he kept buying tax lots for as low as twenty-five or fifty dollars, and these had gone up radically in value. As I remember, his estate came to about four or five million dollars, and he hadn't made a will.

Needless to say, the Attorney General of California instituted escheat proceedings. Then all of a sudden a bunch of Russians showed up claiming they were remote relatives and thus heirs of John's. The case was tried in the superior court, and the Russians won. John Horman must have turned over in his grave at that decision which wasn't what he wanted at all, but it sure made a bunch of Russians happy.

Dick Richard

Before anyone gets the idea that early Newport consisted entirely of barflies, I hasten to mention that it was the birthplace of the present business and commercial development of this city. At a time when Balboa was living on bootleg liquor, illegal gambling and a dance hall, when city officials were trying to sell all the tax lots in Corona del Mar to Joe Rossi for $10,000, and a reluctant Balboa Island was being dragged kicking and screaming by Joe Beek into a recognizable community, Newport was beginning to show the kind of community leadership that was to bring this town into its present position as one of the most desirable living spots on the globe and one of the most aggressive financial centers in the country.

Lew Wallace founded the first bank in the history of the City of Newport Beach right there on the oceanfront not far from the present Blackie's Beer Joint. Unfortunately, Mr. Wallace's bank went belly up during the Depression to be replaced by–what else?–a saloon, Beddome's. Unhappily, the new saloon didn't fare any better than Mr. Wallace's bank. The competition from Stark's and the Stag drove it out of business.

To me, the man who best epitomizes the spirit of old Newport was Dick Richard.

The first time I ever saw Dick Richard he was almost bouncing up and down with energy as he stood on the sidewalk in front of Loy's Market on Oceanfront in Newport. Dick worked at the market, but instead of staying beside the cash register as did most market employees Dick went out on the sidewalk where he shook hands with all passersby as he tried to herd them into the market. His energy was irresistible.

This energy caught the eye of the Griffith Company which owned most of Lido Isle, and that company backed Dick in the construction of Richard's Market at the entrance to that island. And what a market it was! People came from miles around to gawk at it. It was years ahead of its time, the first real upscale market in Southern California. The wise guys said it wouldn't last a year. It made a million dollars that first year.

In his new market Dick found himself cheek by jowl with Paul Palmer and his Newport Balboa Savings and Loan Association. Those two entrepreneurs put their heads together and created the first upscale shopping center in the country at the entrance of Lido Isle, a model for all present-day shopping centers.

But Dick Richard was much more than a successful businessman. He was a great community leader. He could have been elected to anything but assiduously stayed out of politics. He was active in the Newport Harbor Chamber of Commerce, eventually its president, and today a bust of Dick Richard graces the office of the Chamber of Commerce. He was the first president of the Orange County Philharmonic Society, a leader in the Boy Scouts, the Boys Club, the United Fund–just about every worthwhile community activity.

Quite a guy, Dick Richard, but I still remember him best bouncing up and down with barely repressed energy in front of Loy's Market on Oceanfront in old Newport.

Blind Mullet

I think the true essence of old Newport was its pier. The story of McFadden's Wharf has been told and retold in every history of Newport Beach, and I don't need to retell it here. However, a good way to compare Newport and Balboa is to compare their piers. Since Balboa Island didn't face the ocean, it had no pier. Corona del Mar had one very briefly at Main Beach, but it lasted too short a time to be of much interest. But Balboa had a pier, and the two piers–the one in Newport and the one in Balboa–are good reflections of the two communities.

The Newport pier, successor to McFadden's Wharf, was a commercial pier. The Balboa pier was a tourist pier. Thus the Balboa pier had railings so that tourists could lean against them while admiring the beautiful blue Pacific Ocean. The Newport pier had no railings. When ships tied up to load and unload, railings would have been a nuisance. Even when McFadden's Wharf became the Newport pier and ships no longer tied up to it and trains no longer came out on the tracks, the Newport pier had no railings. If a tourist fell off the pier while admiring the beautiful blue Pacific Ocean that was just too bad. Oh, later, much later, they put railings on the Newport pier, but it is best remembered as having no railings. So the Balboa pier had railings, the

Newport pier didn't.

Then the Newport pier had a railroad line running the length of the pier. The Balboa pier not only didn't have a railroad line, the closest thing to a railroad was the Pacific Electric line which stopped a couple of blocks from that pier. So, the Newport pier had a railroad line. The Balboa pier didn't.

Also, the Newport pier was higher and immeasurably more sturdy than the Balboa pier. It had to be to handle that railroad and all those ships. Let's face it. The Balboa pier was pretty rickety. It couldn't have handled an automobile let alone a railroad engine.

Of course, we Balboans thought our pier was higher than it actually was. Whenever big surf came the Balboa pier was closed because with every big wave about six inches of water came rushing down the floor of the pier. We all claimed the Balboa pier was a twenty-foot pier. That made the waves twenty-foot monsters. When you took off you glanced to your right, and if you saw water running down the floor of the pier you said to yourself, "Man, I'm riding a twenty-foot wave." Nonsense. Maybe the Balboa pier was twenty feet above the water line at extreme low tide but not at any other time. As the world now knows, twenty-foot waves occur in very few places in the world. The Balboa pier wasn't one of those places. On the other hand, the Newport pier was high, twenty feet above the water line at all times. It had to be to handle the loading and unloading of people and cargo. I've never met anyone yet who claims he saw water running down the floor of the Newport pier, at least not until the 1939 chubasco which wiped out a lot of piers in Southern California, and if my recollection is right, knocked the end off the Newport pier. It demolished the Balboa pier. So, the Newport pier was strong and high. The Balboa pier was neither.

But the real difference between the two piers was their toilet facilities. If, while strolling on the Balboa pier, one felt the need to go to the toilet, quite a challenge was presented. Hopefully, one was not in too much of a hurry. First one had to walk back to the foot of the pier at Main Street. Then one walked–or ran–two blocks down Main Street toward the Pavilion. When one came to Soto's Curio Shop at the corner of Main Street and Bay Avenue, one turned to the left and walked another block to the corner of Bay Avenue and Washington Street. There one found a small cement structure bearing a sign which read, "Public Comfort Station." That was the public toilet.

I have always thought the sign "Comfort Station" was more accurate than the sign that replaced it which read "Public Restroom." One usually gets a certain degree of comfort while utilizing such a place, but one does not necessarily get much rest.

On the other hand, the Newport pier, as a commercial pier, had its own toilet/comfort station/restroom right there on the pier. The reason was obvious. The Newport pier was a commercial pier. The idea of having workmen who were being paid by the hour taking time off at the employer's expense to leave the pier in search of a toilet/comfort station/restroom on the shore was simply unacceptable to the employers who, after all, owned the pier. Thus, the Newport pier had its own toilet/comfort station/restroom there on the pier.

However, since there was no sewer line running out on the Newport pier, it had for its toilet/comfort station/restroom an old fashioned privy, an outhouse, a structure enclosing and supporting a board containing a hole large enough to sit on and do whatever one does in a privy/outhouse/comfort station/restroom.

In a society which has a hard enough time saying the word toilet, trying to describe in words acceptable to the general public just what is deposited in such a toilet presents a challenge. However . . .

In the traditional privy or outhouse which is ordinarily built over a hole in the ground, that which is deposited through that hole in the board is deposited into that hole in the ground. The Newport pier had no such hole in the ground. Whatever went through that hole in the board in the privy/outhouse/comfort station/restroom went plop right into the beautiful blue Pacific Ocean. So far, so good. However, those unmentionable objects floated ashore where the happy bathers were frolicking in the surf. The local Newport kids, mostly children of fishermen, called those unmentionable objects blind mullet.

Now before the inhabitants of Balboa and Balboa Island become too outraged at the concept of raw sewage being deposited in the water in such a way that it may come in contact with swimmers, let me hasten to add that early Balboa and Balboa Island faced the same problem.

Balboa and Balboa Island being built practically at sea level couldn't have outhouses. Try to dig a hole in the ground in Balboa or Balboa Island and you get water almost immediately. So early Balboa and Balboa Island had sewers. But their sewers emptied right into the bay at the end of each street. Obviously, the same unmentionable objects that floated ashore from the Newport pier also floated ashore in the bay at Balboa and Balboa Island. Joe Beek mentions this problem with great delicacy in his fascinating book Balboa Island Yarns. "The sewers emptied on the beach at street ends. At high tide this condition was not apparent, but at low water it was all too evident."

I would add that at high tide or low tide the problem was apparent to swimmers in the bay, particularly at the beach where I learned to swim, the beach then called the White Bridge Beach, now known as the Montero Street Beach. There the sewers from Montero Street, Anade Street and Alvarado Street on the Balboa side poured into the narrow channel between that beach and Bay Island. At the same time the sewage from Bay Island poured into that same narrow channel.

And so it was that those of us who learned to swim at that beach learned to dog paddle or do the breast stroke so we could watch ahead for anything suspicious that happened to be floating in the water ahead of us. We also learned to keep our mouths tightly closed while swimming.

SO THERE YOU HAVE IT. . .

So there you have it, early Newport, warts, wrinkles and all as demanded by Oliver Cromwell.

I guess I was a little thoughtless when I labeled early Newport as a drab fishing village. Any town that has given us Dollar Dolly, Deefy Johnson and blind mullet can't be all bad.

And so to Balboa Island . . .

ALBOA YACHT BASIN
BALBOA
EACON BAY
NORTH BAY FRONT
10
BRIDGE
MARINE
GRAND
ONYX
AMETHYST
APOLENA
CORAL
SAPPHIRE
DIAMOND
RUBY
COLLINS
ABALONE
CANAL
BALBOA AVE
NORTH BALBOA AVE
BALBOA ISLAND
PARK
PEARL
AGATE
OPAL
TOPAZ
TURQUOISE
AVE
SOUTH BAY FRONT
BULKHEAD LINE
PIER
CHANNEL
10
RBOR MASTER

BALBOA ISLAND

Book Two

BALBOA ISLAND

If I had a rather condescending attitude toward Balboa Island in *Bawdy Balboa*, it came from the contrasting lifestyles. Balboa was a rude, crude, noisy, honky-tonk resort. Balboa Island was quiet, staid, respectable–a bedroom community. I suppose that one reared in the early West in Dodge City or Tombstone would find Mingo, Iowa, a little dull, just as one reared on Bourbon Street in New Orleans would find life in an Amish village downright dreary. Apparently my jaundiced view of Balboa Island was shared by others. When faced with the request of Balboa Island to be annexed to the City of Newport Beach, the then-mayor said, "Balboa Island is a dump. It was sold by a bunch of crooks to a lot of damned fools."

There's A There There

In *Bawdy Balboa* I described Balboa Island as a "mud flat with mosquitoes." In Jim Felton's Newport Beach 75, Bill Grundy describes it as a "marshy sandbar." But mud flat or marshy sandbar, I'll stand by my statement that the place had mosquitoes. It was those mosquitoes that caused Tagg Atwood, Spenny Richardson and me to borrow Joe Beek's Balboa Island ferry one night just to escape those pesky critters.

The ferry ceased operation at midnight. After that hour, a practice had evolved by which one stranded on the wrong side of the bay would simply walk along the bayfront until one found a rowboat that one would row across. The next morning, Tommy Bouchey, the harbor master, would cruise along picking up rowboats and returning them to their proper locations. It was a nice practice.

And so it happened that Tagg, Spenny and I found ourselves stranded on Balboa Island after the ferry had quit its regular run. Nothing daunted, we went up and down the bayfront looking for a rowboat. Apparently, the Balboa Island half of the old lend/lease had gone out of style. Each and every rowboat was locked and chained.

The mosquitoes were fierce. We were ready to do anything to get off that island–even swim. We were sitting on the ferry preparatory to shucking our clothes and swimming over when I happened to look at the wheelhouse, and lo and behold, the operator had left the key in the ignition. Tagg turned the key, and the motor rumbled into action. Our only thought was putting as much distance between ourselves and those mosquitoes, so we cast off and didn't think about what we'd done until we'd left the pests behind and were nearly on the other side. That's when we heard the sirens and began to think about the situation. It was low tide, and as we put the ferry into the slip, we jumped off into the mud and hunkered under the wharf. The police came, walked around on the wharf, but for some reason didn't shine their lights down on the mud. After a while they left and we crawled out, covered with slime but safe from both the mosquitoes and the police, or so I thought. Later, Joe Beek mentioned it in his book, so I guess our little escapade didn't go undetected.

As a child, all I knew about Balboa Island was that it was across the bay, and that on the Fourth of July everyone on the Balboa side shot skyrockets toward Balboa Island trying to burn the place down. That was the extent of my consideration. Then something happened that colored my thinking about the place.

I was going through my Tarzan stage. Playing Tarzan was tough enough in Wyoming where I had lived before coming to Balboa, with only sagebrush to climb while waiting to pounce on Numa the lion. In Balboa, it was even more difficult with no trees and not even any sagebrush, so I ran over the roofs of the houses of the summer visitors. That was all right during the winter, but when summer came, the summer visitors took a dim view of some kid running over their roofs. At the time, I thought those summer visitors were pretty unreasonable although in retrospect I must admit it must have been disconcerting to be having lunch with the family and hear some ten-year-old kid clatter over the roof and leap down on the family cat screaming, "Numa! You die!"

One summer day, banned from the roofs, I was walking down Central Avenue near the library when a big car pulled up and stopped. A voice said, "Son, can you direct me to the Balboa Island ferry?"

I looked up and my heart almost stopped. It was Elmo Lincoln! For the uninitiated, Elmo Lincoln was the first movie Tarzan. Mr. Lincoln was a rather rotund man who stalked around on the screen wearing a lionskin cape and carrying a spear. With that spear he killed countless natives while saving Jane. Since those were silent films, we never heard him let out the kind of scream made famous by a later Tarzan, one Johnny Weissmuller. Neither did Mr. Lincoln dive into the water and wrestle with crocodiles. Mr. Lincoln was no Olympic champion, and as far as I know he couldn't even swim. Neither did he swing from handy vines on jungle trees. I'll wager a guess that Mr. Lincoln couldn't even climb a tree. Actually, all I can remember him doing was stalking–almost strutting–around in that lionskin cape carrying that spear. Be that as it may, he was Tarzan and thus my boyhood hero.

In reply to his question I stammered out directions. Mr. Lincoln thanked me and took off. I raced after him as fast as my spindly legs would carry me. Alas, I got there too late. The ferry was just pulling out with Elmo Lincoln's car as its only passenger.

I waited all day there at the ferry landing for Mr. Lincoln to return. He never did. I know now that there was a bridge on the other side of the island over which Mr. Lincoln undoubtedly escaped. Anyway, he didn't return on the ferry, and I think I always held a secret grudge against Balboa Island for having swallowed my hero.

Another negative was that everyone said Balboa Island was under water most of the time. I realize now that this was a bit of an exaggeration. However, in its early days, before the present bulkhead was constructed, Balboa Island was almost completely immersed at high tide. In Balboa they said the expression "The whole town's under water" was coined for Balboa Island. Not that Balboa was without its own water problems. It got flooded any time big surf combined with high tides. I can remember taking off on a big wave at high tide next to the Balboa pier and looking down Main Street and seeing some guy rowing down the street toward the Pavilion.

I suppose the other thing was that Balboa Island just seemed so quiet in comparison to Balboa.

In those early days, Main Street in Balboa surged with a noisy, ribald crowd on Saturday night. The same Saturday night you could shoot a Gatling gun down Marine Avenue on Balboa Island and never endanger a soul.

Balboa never had less than three wide-open gambling joints collecting money from the suckers. Balboa Island didn't even have church-sponsored bingo.

During Prohibition days, Balboa had its justly famous Drugless Drugstore where one couldn't buy as much as an aspirin tablet but one could get illegal straight alcohol across the counter for two bits an ounce. Not only was Balboa Island's pharmacy on the up-and-up, the place didn't even have a bootlegger. After the repeal of Prohibition, while Balboa never had less than six bars, Balboa Island never had more than one, not even to this day.

What Balboa Island did have was people. As the mosquito population dwindled, the people population surged. Balboa Island grew and grew and grew until today you can't find a parking place on the Island except maybe on a dreary day in February.

What Balboa Island also had was boats. Balboa lived on Main Street and the ocean. Since Balboa Island didn't have either a Main Street or an ocean, it turned to the bay and boats, lots of boats. Every kid on the island had a boat. Sea Sleds, Runabouts, Sabots, Bay Sloops, Flappers, R Boats Sand Dabs, Sand Dollars, Sea Mews, Skimmers, and, of course, Snow Birds and Star Boats. They had races on races.

So, I guess there was a there there. Not as noisy as Balboa but still interesting. And in all honesty, I really can't blame Balboa Island because Elmo Lincoln didn't come back. He was probably buying a lot from W. S. Collins.

Berry Ruth Mrs h 124 Onyx av Balboa Island
Bertrand Jas W (Blanche E) 108 Via Trieste Lido Isle
Bertrand M H (LA) 213 19th st Newport
Bertuleit Walter (LA) 220 Pearl av Balboa Island
Biane M (Ontario) 1113 W Central av Newport
Bickel Chester h 410 Poinsettia av Corona del Mar
Bidwell R B (Glendora) 122 Garnet av Balboa Island
Bidwell R W (Pasadena) 206 Sapphire av Balboa Island
Bieler Hal Dr (Altadena) 512 Ocean blvd Corona del Mar
Bill Mae M tchr High Schl r 106 Coral av Balboa Island
Bill's Coffee Shop (W F Ireland) 108 Main st Balboa
Binford E M (LA) 308 E Surf Balboa
Binley N O (Pasadena) 210 Ruby av Balboa Island
Bird Hulda Mrs h 214 36th st Newport
Birmeier Cliff waiter Gus' r 301½ Main st Balboa
Bishop Annie Mrs r 219 29th st Newport
Bishop E J (Rebecca E) h 1407 N Bay Fr Balboa Island
Bishop J O (Glendale) 116 Ruby av Balboa Island
Bittner Henry r 628 Clubhouse av Newport
Bittner Tom r 628 Clubhouse av Newport
Black Wm Mrs (LA) 212 Abalone av Balboa Island
BLACKBEARD S W (Thelma) Electrical Contractor ofc
    325 Santa Ana av Newport Heights—22, h same
Blackburn John (Norwalk) 5308 Ocean Fr Newport
Blackburn Ralph (Edna) r 230½ Pearl av Balboa Island
Blackburn Wm J (Florence) rnchr h 5308 Ocean Fr Nwpt
Blackshare Doris slsldy Ida Naylor's r 202½ Apolena av
    Balboa Island
Blackstock Jess (Vera) boatmn r 1914 Court av Newport
Blaich W F—Mariam (Whittier) 1319 E Central Balboa
Blair Miss r 400 E Central av Balboa
Blair Russell (LA) 222 Opal av Balboa Island
Blake F A (Orange) 318 Anade av Balboa
Blake F O (Whittier) 1008 S Bay Fr Balboa Island
Blake I B (LA) 813 W Central av Balboa
Blake R G shows h 617 Heliotrope av Corona del Mar

In The Beginning

A man named William S. Collins founded Balboa Island. I regret that I never met Mr. Collins. He must have been the ultimate promoter. He and P. T. Barnum should have been partners. It is reported that he was very handsome. He was also obviously charming, smooth and convincing. And it goes without saying that he had the nerves of a Mississippi river boat gambler.

While still in his thirties, he surfaced in Southern California from a somewhat murky background in Arizona–oil wells, gold mines, subdivisions, a savings and loan company, whatever.

The first thing he did was buy from James McFadden in 1902 all of the present City of Newport Beach from the Santa Ana River to 9th Street in Balboa. He got it for $70.00 an acre. It has been reported that McFadden boasted that he had duped a sucker. Actually, McFadden never knew what hit him.

Collins promptly subdivided his newly acquired property and began selling lots to those who had been merely squatters on the McFadden land. Soon Collins had his money back. He then went into partnership with Henry Huntington, nephew of Collis Huntington of Southern Pacific Railway fame. Collins made Henry Huntington a partner in his new Newport Beach Company for $37,500 in cash and a promise to bring Huntington's Pacific Electric Railway to Newport Beach. The P. E. and its big red cars already criss-crossed most of Southern California. To get the P. E. to Newport Beach, Collins had to give Huntington a 100-foot right-of-way through Newport plus a big mud flat called Electric Island. While Electric Island was practically worthless as a mud flat, with a little artful dredging it became Lido Isle.

Once the Pacific Electric arrived in Newport, the promoters of Balboa and East Newport situated farther down the peninsula wanted a piece of the action, too. They got it–for $19,000 in cash plus a right-of-way from McFadden Square in Newport to Main Street in Balboa.

William S. Collins was off and running.

He next surfaces in 1904 as the owner and operator of a machine shop in Balboa where he built a small dredger with which he was eventually to build Balboa Island. This machine shop evolved into the area's first boatyard. However, operating a boatyard must have seemed pretty drab to the flamboy-ant Mr. Collins. He got into speedboats. He announced he was going to dredge a motorboat raceway around what was eventually to become Balboa Island. He never did. Instead, he bought a fast hydroplane he called the Balboa Island Flyer II (there never was a Balboa Island Flyer I) and drove it around the bay at speeds up to sixty miles an hour. The noise from this motorboat drove all the inhabitants of the peninsula crazy with its thunderous roar. Then, just to outdo himself, he built a fifty-one foot motor cruiser which he named the W. S. (his initials). This was the largest and fastest boat in the bay. William S. Collins would have no less.

During this period, he also opened a bank. To the surprise of no one except the credulous depositors it closed a year later, and just what happened to the deposits is not recorded.

Also during this period he disposed of all his real estate holdings on the peninsula, probably to pay for his speedboat hobby. He now turned his attention to what eventually became Balboa Island.

The mud flat/sandy marsh was not known originally as Balboa Island. Its first name was Snipe Island, named after a particularly hardy shorebird. It had to be hardy to live with all those mosquitoes. The next name was Crusoe Island, obviously named after Defoe's Robinson Crusoe. Tradition has it that some poor wretch spent a night on the mud flat/marshy sandbar with all those mosquitoes and announced that even Robinson Crusoe couldn't live on that desolate, mosquito-infested piece of mud. Somewhere along the line it also had been known as Newport Island although the McFaddens, founders of Newport Beach, disclaimed any connection with the place. They had plenty of mud flats and marshy sandbars of their own.

Collins rejected all these names and called it Balboa Island, a name with a certain staying power since it has lasted down to modern times.

As Collins surveyed his newly-named island, he observed that most of it was under water at high tide. With the handy little dredger he had built in his machine shop he filled in the low places and began to sell lots "with all improvements in and paid for." Whether paid for or not, the improvements consisted of a sewer system in which the sewers emptied into the bay at street ends (shades of Newport and its blind mullet) and an almost useless bulkhead which merely kept water out long enough to sell lots.

Collins advertised his inside lots for $350 and the bayfront lots for $650-750. He put on trips from Los Angeles to Balboa by P. E. and across the bay on his rather primitive ferry–he had secured the first ferry permit in 1909–all this plus a free lunch, of course. He also made a few rash promises. He promised a fine concrete bridge to the mainland. Instead he built a ramshackle twelve-foot wooden bridge. He promised an eight-car ferry which has not materialized to this day. He promised a 150-room hotel which was simply a pipe dream.

Two things he did do. He sold lots, and he built a concrete castle for his wife on the western tip of the island. As the world knows, Balboa Island, like Caesar's Gaul, is divided into three parts. There is the main island. To the east there is the Little Island separated from the main island by the so-called Grand Canal which is neither grand nor much of a canal at low tide. On the western tip there is a small island that he named Collins Island. There he built the castle for his fourth wife, Apolena.

However, for a promoter, life has its ups and downs, even for a superlative one like William S. Collins. By 1915 he had lost all his holdings on Balboa Island except Apolena's castle, and lots were going for as little as twenty-five dollars.

Shortly thereafter, William S. Collins left town, and just where he went seems to be somewhat of a mystery. It is rumored that he went into the High Sierras where he subdivided and sold mountain meadows and didn't have to worry about high and low tides. Whether the rumor is true or not, I have a hunch that when the big Florida land boom of the 1920s came along and promoters were selling lots during the low tide because they were covered with water during high tide, William S. Collins wasn't too far away.

William S. Collins left his mark on Balboa Island. Not only did he leave Collins Island and Collins Avenue he also left Apolena Street. How many others in the history of this town have left an island and a street named after themselves plus a street named after his wife–particularly his fourth wife?

Joe Beek

Ihave an unfortunate tendency to be a little irreverent when talking about people and things. Not when it comes to Joe Beek. I stand in awe of the man and his accomplishments. I once said that the two most important things that ever happened on Balboa Island were Joe Beek and the Balboa Island Punting and Sculling Society. Not bad. Perhaps a touch of hyperbole but basically sound.

Joe Beek first surfaced as a young graduate of Pasadena's Throop Institute, now Cal Tech. The flamboyant W. S. Collins hired the young man to build a bridge connecting Balboa Island to the mainland. Oh, it wasn't the great, wide concrete structure of Mr. Collins's extravagant claims. Nevertheless, it was a bridge, a narrow wooden structure and the first structure connecting Balboa Island to the mainland. After he completed the bridge, Joe Beek was off and running.

His accomplishments were nothing less than amazing. He became the town's first harbor master. An ardent yachtsman, he was an early Commodore of the Newport Harbor Yacht Club and one of the organizers of the Balboa Yacht Club. He was on the first library board, was on the first Newport Harbor High School board. He was one of the founders of the Newport-Balboa

Federal Savings and Loan Association. For many years he was Secretary of the California State Senate. He was the developer of Beacon Bay and Harbor Island. The list goes on and on. However, a few things stand out.

THE BALBOA ISLAND FERRY

While Mr. Collins had secured a permit from the city to operate a ferry from Balboa to Balboa Island, he did practically nothing about it. Then Joe Beek secured such a permit, and the real saga of the Balboa Island ferry began. His first ferryboat was a clumsy outboard named the Ark. It carried oars just in case the outboard gave out. This was followed by ferries bearing such names as the Fat Ferry, the Joker and many others. Along the way Joe had the ferry declared a public utility, probably the smallest one in the state. In its early days, Joe being Joe did his own dredging for the ferry landing. This didn't mean operating some large mechanical dredger by himself. He would wade out, fill a dredge bucket by hand, then turn it over to his wife, Carol, who hauled it in and dumped it to fill out the landing. The Balboa Island ferry is still a Beek family operated enterprise, but I am not aware that the family still does its own dredging.

THE CHUBASCO

Joe was a superlative boat handler. When a chubasco roared without warning out of the Gulf of California on September 20, 1939, Joe was in Santa Monica. He started for home in his boat, the Vamos. The chubasco hit, destroying piers and capsizing boats caught in the Catalina channel. Joe rescued several boats and their occupants that dreadful day.

CAPTAIN BEEK

Came World War II and Joe was too old for the military. Not to worry. He had a birth certificate forged. This showed him to be several years younger than he actually was. He then went into the Army Transport Service which had a fleet of small freighters. Joe became a four-striper, a captain no less. He started across the Pacific with a flotilla of these small craft, and by the time they arrived on the other side he had become the commodore of the flotilla because of his outstanding seamanship.

THE BALBOA ISLAND YACHT CLUB

I think that the accomplishment of which Joe Beek was most proud was the founding, again with Carol, of the Balboa Island Yacht Club, a club for youngsters six to sixteen. There they taught seamanship, boat handling, sailing, swimming, water sports, and most of all, good citizenship. That club is now over seventy years of age, and during that seventy years has turned out some of the outstanding leaders of this community.

THE MOUNTAIN MEADOW

A little known part of the Joe Beek saga is his mountain retreat. Somehow, he had acquired a square mile of land in the mountains between the city of Corona and Black Star Canyon in Orange County. Here he could exercise that eager, inquiring mind. He drilled a well and planted many species of evergreen trees, a particular hobby of his. He installed one of the earliest wind-driven generators which furnished electricity for the place. I can visualize Joe Beek sitting on a boulder in his mountain retreat, eyes focused on something in the distance, and saying to himself, "What will I do next?"

I suppose his ultimate triumph was picking up the pieces of the shambles left by William S. Collins of that mud flat/marshy sandbar called Balboa Island. Oh, Joe didn't do it all by himself. A lot of people pitched in. The island had its ups and downs even after Collins left. But it was Joe Beek's persistence, his energy that was the driving force behind the resurrection of Balboa Island and its development into what it is today, a little crowded, but one of the most desirable places to live in the whole country. It owes a lot to Joe Beek.

WWII

It is commonly believed that the only military establishments in Orange County during World War II were the Marine Corps Air Station in El Toro, the Lighter Than Air Base in Tustin, the Los Alamitos Navy Air Station in Los Alamitos, and the Seal Beach Ammunition Station in Seal Beach. Not so. Newport Beach had its own military establishment, a United States Coast Guard Patrol Station located where? On Balboa Island. More specifically on Collins Island in the castle built by Mr. Collins for his wife, Apolena.

It is difficult to visualize today, in the light of after events, the hysteria caused in this part of the country by the Japanese attack on Pearl Harbor. As far as Californians were concerned, the next step of the Japanese war machine was, quite logically, the coast of California. While we now know that the sole attack on our shores was the night a Japanese submarine surfaced near Santa Barbara and lobbed a few shells at some oil rigs in Goleta, at that time California could visualize Japanese soldiers storming ashore at almost any place along the coast. Foxholes were dug on the bluffs from Corona del Mar to Laguna. A powerful searchlight was mounted on the end of the Huntington Beach pier. Preparations were commenced for the installation of coast artillery on the bluffs back of Bolsa Chica. Every night householders who had been looking for years at the ocean break on a rock off Laguna or San Clemente called the authorities to report a Japanese submarine surfacing there. Militia companies were formed. A blackout was enforced along the coast. Even after it was pretty obvious that the war was being fought in such far-off places as Guadalcanal, Tarawa, Saipan and Okinawa, California kept itself in a state of military preparedness. And part of that preparedness was the Coast Guard Patrol Station, Newport Beach, which just happened to be located on Collins Island.

Long Beach, San Pedro and San Diego were the logical places for our naval forces. However, where better a place for patrolling the coast than half-way between Long Beach and San Diego? Also Newport Beach and its fishing fleet had to continue fishing to feed the populace, and they had to be checked coming and going for the possibility that one of those fishing boats might meet a Japanese submarine and acquire a saboteur to land and play havoc with our military installations.

Thus a barge was stationed in the channel mouth. There the Coast Guard checked all craft coming into and going out of the harbor. There was some talk of a submarine net across the channel, but wiser heads prevailed. It would have to be a mighty small submarine to get into the channel mouth, and once in, what would it torpedo–the Balboa Island ferry?

It was from that barge that one of the great but untold stories of our war in the Pacific unfolds.

The Navy was in the process of acquiring yachts up and down the coast, bringing them into one of our brand new shipyards, painting them gray and sending them out to patrol the Catalina channel. It didn't hurt, and it kept a lot of people busy.

And so it was that the Great Confrontation between the United States Navy and the United States Coast Guard occurred right there in the channel mouth leading into Newport Harbor. It involved two ensigns, one from the Coast Guard and one from the Navy, each dressed in his brand new uniform, each sporting that one stripe on his sleeve in jazzy gold. I shall call the one from the Coast Guard Ensign White, the one from the Navy Ensign Black.

Ensign Black, USNR, came steaming into Newport Harbor on a small yacht the Navy had acquired in San Diego. He was on his way to the South Coast Shipyard where this nice white yacht would be painted gray and become an integral part of the United States Navy.

On the barge protecting Newport Harbor from the enemy was Ensign White, USCGR. As Ensign Black came alongside, Ensign White ordered him to stop for inspection.

No way, said Ensign Black. He was an officer of the United States Navy, and no two-bit Coast Guard officer was going to stop him as he carried out his United States naval duties. The U.S.S. Saratoga would certainly not stop for any piddling inspection. Neither would he. He steamed grandly past the barge.

Thunderstruck at such a breach of security, Ensign White leaped into his patrol boat which was tied up at the barge and started up the bay in hot pursuit of Ensign Black. Coming alongside, he ordered Ensign Black to heave to or whatever salty language a Coast Guard officer uses to tell a boat to stop.

Ensign Black would have no part of this. In the great tradition of the Navy, damn the torpedoes, or in this case, the Coast Guard, full speed ahead.

Ensign White ordered his crew of two enlisted Coast Guard seamen to prepare to board.

Ensign Black ordered his crew of two enlisted men to prepare to repel boarders.

Ensign White, in tones that would have made John Paul Jones proud, shouted to his crew, "Board!"

Ensign Black, in tones that would have satisfied Stephen Decatur, yelled to his crew, "Repel boarders!"

Despite the orders, no boarding or repelling took place. The four crewmen were giggling too hard to do anything.

When the two boats arrived at the South Coast Boatyard, each made numerous charges against the other, but the only outcome was that Ensign Black was transferred to a Naval Recruiting Station in Dubuque, and Ensign White was transferred to similar Coast Guard duty in Kalamazoo.

As William Tecumseh Sherman said, "War is hell."

Just A Bunch Of Rich Drunks

The Balboa Island Punting and Sculling Society was born in Art White's Park Avenue Cafe and Bar, located at the corner of Marine and Park on Balboa Island. Someone owned the place before Art White, but intensive research fails to identify him, this research consisting of conversations with Bill Lester who boasts that he is the only person to have worked at all four corners of Marine and Park. He worked for John Allen in the drugstore, for Tony Hershey in the market. He worked for Matt Cox in the service station. He worked for whoever it was that had the cafe and bar before Art White acquired it, but he can't remember the guy's name. So much for deep research.

Art and Vaux White were brothers who came to Balboa in the early days and took over Young's Cafe at the corner of Main and Central, the present location of Dillman's. They broke up. Art moved to Balboa Island. Vaux stayed in Balboa, and his cafe, Vaux's, became very much a part of the town's early history. The most intriguing aspect of that operation was the domed circular bar. That dome had certain acoustical qualities by which something whispered at one part of the bar was heard distinctly by the person sitting directly across the circular bar from the speaker or, in many cases, the whisperer. This quality in the bar led to some serious confrontations as supposedly secret and often scurrilous comments about the person sitting across the bar were heard distinctly by that person. But enough of Vaux. He belongs to Balboa.

Art acquired the bar on Balboa Island, the only one then and now on the island. I guess it's written in the city charter that there can be only one bar on Balboa Island. Art's bar soon acquired a loyal following. I was living temporarily on the island while I was building a home in Corona del Mar and would see the serious drinkers lined up in the bar each morning when I went to work. Then in the evening when I returned it seemed to me that the same bunch were lined up in the same seats at the same bar. That's loyalty. Or the result of having only one bar on the island.

Among those who were in regular attendance at the Park Avenue Bar were cartoonists Virgil Partch and Dick Shaw. They became the leaders of a group of fellow drinkers, and one night they decided to form a club. They named it the Balboa Island Punting and Sculling Society.

Fortunately for history, Chuck Masters is in possession of the original menu on which the founding members of the organization inscribed their names, just like the Declaration of Independence: Art White, Pinky Scott, Chuck Masters, Crel Griffith, Bob Anderson, Rob Lewis, Gordie Weevil, Jim Barrett, Al Payne and, of course, Virgil Partch and Dick Shaw–all names known in drinking circles but names not necessarily found in any formal history of Newport Beach.

When asked to describe the organization, Virgil Partch, who always had a way with words, said, "Just a bunch of rich drunks."

This bunch might have toiled in obscurity had not someone come up with a splendid idea. Why not sail a boat from Balboa Island to Las Vegas? The search for fame and fortune was on.

Somehow they got a forty-foot cabin cruiser aboard a flatbed truck and took off. The cruiser was well equipped with the necessary liquid refreshments. It was a long trip. This was before the freeway, and the trip usually took about five hours. The trip of the Balboa Island Punting and Sculling Society took somewhat longer. Its members lasted as far as the Cajon pass between San Bernardino and Barstow before they made their first stop at a friendly neighborhood watering hole to spread the gospel of their club. Several other stops were made at desert bars. Apparently word spread that they were coming because when they arrived in Las Vegas the town's public relations staff was in full cry. They were met with everything but a tickertape parade.

By the time they arrived, someone had conceived of the brilliant idea of unloading the cruiser into the swimming pool of one of the larger Las Vegas hotels. The patrons and owners of the hotel were delighted with the idea. Unhappily, nothing came of this aspect of the trip because the cement around the pool began to crack with the weight of the truck and the yacht. Nevertheless, the trip was a howling success, and the Balboa Island Punting and Sculling Society became a household name across the nation.

Flush with the success of the boat trip to Las Vegas, the club came up with a new idea, a train trip to Catalina. First the members acquired an old-fashioned observation car, complete with bar, of course. However, getting the car to Catalina presented a logistics problem that dwarfed the cruiser-on-a-flatbed truck concept of the Las Vegas adventure. Getting a huge barge on which to load the observation car wasn't too difficult. Neither was there any problem in finding a tug to pull the barge to Catalina. However, it seemed that the Coast Guard took a dim view of a railroad car being towed to Catalina on a barge without some safety measure being taken to keep the observation car from slipping off the barge and drowning the occupants. Under Coast Guard guidance, the car was shored up so that it wouldn't slide off the barge in case they hit bad weather.

Came the day of the event, the media coverage outdid that of the boat trip to Las Vegas. They took off, this time with Balboa's slot machine king, Clyde Denlinger, as Commodore. It was a long trip and not nearly as much fun as the Las Vegas adventure. No stopping at friendly watering holes along the way. Just the damned observation car and miles and miles of dreary salt water. Not one member of the club could be persuaded to make the return trip on the observation car. They all flew home instead. History does not record the final disposition of the observation car and its trusty barge.

After the train-to-Catalina scam, the Balboa Island Punting and Sculling Society lapsed into comparative obscurity until the advent of the Michigan.

The Good Ship Michigan

The origins of the good ship *Michigan* and its connection with the Balboa Island Punting and Sculling Society are shrouded in the mists of legend. The prevailing version has it that one day Virgil Partch and Dick Shaw were walking along the bayfront after having spent a few constructive hours in the Snug Harbor bar when they came upon a sunken boat. Only the superstructure showed. They went back to the Snug Harbor and debated this great discovery, and from that debate, which probably ranks in historical importance with the Lincoln-Douglas debates, they decided to float the boat with the intent of eventually acquiring it. They did, and they did. That is, they got it afloat and acquired it. The sunken boat turned out to be an ancient Monterey-type fishing boat named, for some reason, the *Michigan*. Just how they got it afloat and just from whom they acquired it are not at all clear. Few legends are clear. But I'm a sucker for legends, and I'll stick with this version.

Be that as it may, Partch and Shaw somehow came into possession of the *Michigan*, and she promptly became the flagship of the Balboa Island Punting and Sculling Society and the scene of numerous cocktail cruises. She had one minor fault. She would sink from time to time, but since she never left the harbor, the loss of life from frequent sinkings was negligible although some of the sinkings had a definite sobering-up effect on some of the participants in the cocktail cruises.

Because of the fame of her owners, she became the flagship of several Character Boat Parades until her frequent sinkings caused her retirement from that activity. It put a damper on an affair as well-planned and orchestrated as the Character Boat Parade to have its flagship sink right in the middle of the event.

Time passed, and so did quite a few members of the original group that made up the Balboa Punting and Sculling Society. Partch and Shaw and Chuck Masters and Gordie Weevil were still around, but the rest had gone on to that great cocktail bar in the sky.

Then a man came along who presided over a kind of resurrection of the Society, Bill Veneman.

Bill Veneman was a man with a million ideas, mostly good. He did have a little problem with carrying on with an idea. Just about the time it was beginning to pay off he would get bored and go on to another idea. He was dynamic, energetic, and he reinvigorated the proud tradition of the Balboa Island Punting and Sculling Society when he arranged a race between the good ship *Michigan* and the Coronado ferry owned by the San Diego Rest and Aspiration Society, an organization of hardy souls with social tastes similar to those of the Balboa Island Punting and Sculling Society. They had acquired an old Coronado-San Diego ferry as their flagship on which they took frequent cocktail cruises around San Diego harbor.

Somehow Veneman arranged a race between the two crafts, the race to take place in San Diego Harbor. Of course, the *Michigan* had to be taken down there by truck since she couldn't have gotten as far as Shorecliffs in the open sea, and sinking out there would probably have been the end of that sturdy craft.

The Balboa Island Punting and Sculling Society was, to put it mildly, a very loose-knit group. It never did seem to have a real organization with regular membership, officers and all that jazz. My relationship with the organization was always a little cloudy until one day Partch told me I was its chaplain and that, to coin a phrase, was that. And so it was that I was a participant in the great San Diego race.

The crew of the *Michigan* was to consist of skipper Dick Shaw, Bill Veneman, Chuck Masters, myself and accompanying wives and girlfriends.

The race, from the point of view of the Balboa Island Punting and Sculling Society, was a disaster. The Coronado ferry was a large craft. The poor little *Michigan* wouldn't even have been a lifeboat for that ferry. Also, the ferry could sail along at a pretty good clip. The *Michigan* could barely move–and we always faced the prospect of sinking. Our problems were intensified by the big American flag Dick Shaw had acquired. It was so big that it belonged on a ship the size of the *Queen Mary*. I have never seen such a large American flag. Going into the wind that flag held the *Michigan* dead in the water. Unfortunately for us, the wind was against us in the San Diego race, so for the whole race we barely moved from the starter's gate.

No quitter, in the festivities following the race, Veneman challenged the San Diegans to a return match, this one to be conducted in our harbor. They were overjoyed at an opportunity to embarrass us even more.

So we took the *Michigan* back by truck and waited the rerunning of the Great Race.

Since the San Diegans weren't too sure that their ferry could make the journey from San Diego to Newport Beach, and since it was much too large to put on a truck, they borrowed the *Trojan*, a working tug, from Bill Grundy as their flagship.

The same highly trained professional racing crew that had so gallantly handled the *Michigan* in the San Diego fiasco handled her for this race.

Because of the admitted and proven differences in speeds between the two craft, we were given a small handicap. Since the finish line was at the Balboa Bay Club, we started at the Pavilion. The San Diegans started at the end of the peninsula.

The *Michigan* was in fine fettle. She didn't sink, the engine started without the usual half hour tinkering and swearing and, wonders of wonders, we had a following wind so that the giant flag was not an impediment. Actually, it was a help, just like a sail.

Nevertheless, as we approached the Bay Club, it appeared that another defeat was in the making. The *Trojan* was overtaking us rapidly. She was coming on like a destroyer with a bone in her teeth, as we old Navy people say. Then a miracle occurred.

My wife, Katie, was leaning against a part of the railing of the *Michigan* which was held together by rust, corrosion and oxidized paint. The railing parted, and overboard went Katie.

I suppose that I, as her husband, should have leaped overboard to save her. It never entered my mind. It was winter, the water was cold, and anyway, Katie was a better swimmer than I.

Captain Dick Shaw, who was ordinarily a kind, gentle person, became a kind of modern Captain Bligh when at the wheel of the *Michigan*. He looked down from the so-called wheelhouse, disentangled himself from that huge American flag, said that Katie had a pretty good stroke, and sailed on.

Chuck Masters looked over the rail and said in tones of pure awe, "She hasn't even spilled her drink." That was true. I looked down, and there Katie was, treading water with her glass held high. I have never been more proud of my wife.

The San Diegans, a bit more gallant, stopped to pull Katie out of the water, and this allowed us to cross the finish line ahead, to the enthusiastic cheers of spectators. Race completed, the *Michigan* promptly sank, but by that time her crew, sans Katie, was on its way to the bar.

During the post-race festivities, some of the San Diegans were churlish enough to suggest that we had pushed Katie over. We hadn't, but I am not at all sure that had the thought occurred and the opportunity presented itself, we would have restrained ourselves.

Bowing out at the top of her career, the *Michigan* retired from racing. Somehow she ended up in the possession of Jim Dale, and the last time I saw her she was moored in front of the Villa Nova.

Stag Cafe (Tom Carson) 109 21st pl Newport
Stag Liquor Store (Tom Carson) 2115 Coast blvd Newpt
STAHLER H E DR (Terrell P) dentist ofc Storey Building Balboa—698, h 399 Seville av Balboa—266
Stamp J L (N Hollywood) 227 Coral av Balboa Island
Stanbury Francis T h 202 41st st Newport
Standard Oil Co of Calif Depot (G C Perry slsmn) 18th & W Central av Newport—155
Standard Stations Inc (W J Lewis mgr) Bay Shores
Standlee D M (Puente) 1825 W Central av Newport
Stanford Bishop (Fresno) 201 39th st Newport
Stanford Chas B (Glendale) 901 N Bay Fr Balboa Island
Stanley Earl W (Mildred) real est ofc 410 S Bay Fr Balboa Isl—62-W, r 117 Pearl av Balboa Isl
STANLEY'S GARAGE (E S Burwell) 204 Washington st Balboa—455
Stanley Geo (Pasadena) 117 Pearl av Balboa Island
Stanley Gerold L Mrs (LA) 132 S Bay Fr Balboa Island
Stanley Henry W (LA) 1218 E Surf Balboa
Stanley Irene bkkpr Boomer Building Newport—733
Stanley Mabel Lee Mrs tchr Gram Schl r318 Lindo av Bal
Stanley Silas S (San Berndno) 125 E Central av Balboa
Stans H G (LA) 1532 Miramar dr Balboa
Stansfield R W (Corona) 124 25th st Newport
Starck's Cafe (B O Oquist mgr) 107 21st pl Newport
Starck Elsie Mrs h 1912 Court av Newport
Starck Karl fshmn r 1912 Court av Newport
Starck Marie bkkpr r 1912 Court av Newport
Stasand Geo W (Altdna) 1707 Bay Side dr Corona del Mar
Staunton W F Mrs (LA) 1803 E Bay Fr Balboa—1142
Stauss Edwin R caddymstr Golf Club r 106 29th st Newpt
Stauss Emily H Mrs h 106 29th st Newport
Stayner Clarence (So Pasa) 124 Apolena av Balboa Island
Steadman Geo V (Mae) Falcon Achry r 2304 Ocean Fr Npt

Earl Stanley

The Park Avenue Cafe had two entrances, both facing on Park Avenue. The one nearer Marine Avenue opened into the cafe. The one farther from Marine Avenue was a double door. Go in the left side and you entered the Park Avenue bar. Enter the right side and you went into the real estate office of Earl Stanley.

Earl Stanley was a realtor, a very successful realtor. He also became a politician, a very successful politician, a member of the City Council of Newport Beach and later a member of the Assembly of the State of California.

Earl Stanley was rather short, a trifle rotund, with a ruddy complexion, white hair and a nice, almost bashful smile. He was also a very nice guy.

After World War II and the death of the Balboa political group that had been running the city for the last twenty years, a group of new faces from Balboa Island and Corona del Mar began to emerge as the political leaders of the city. Among them were Clyan Hall and Braden Finch from Corona del Mar, and Bob Allen and Earl Stanley from Balboa Island. All eventually went to the city council, but Earl had the most brilliant political future.

As far as I know Earl Stanley was the only person ever elected to the Newport Beach City Council with the open backing of The Irvine Company.

Ordinarily, Irvine Company sponsorship was the kiss of death.

Old Man Irvine liked Earl Stanley. As a result, Earl got to handle the new Irvine projects of Bay Shores and Cliffhaven. Earl saw no reason to disclaim or hide his relationship with The Irvine Company. However, his open support of the company's plans for the future development of the city put him at odds with the rest of the council members. As a result, Earl was usually on the short end of a four-to-one vote on almost any measure.

Undaunted, Earl Stanley then ran for and was elected to the state Assembly, the first assemblyman from the harbor area or for that matter from the whole coast of the county. He was an instant success in Sacramento, becoming one of the real powers in the legislature, trusted and respected by both Republicans and Democrats.

After a few terms, Earl announced he was not going to run again and returned to Balboa Island to resume his real estate career. He tried to sell me a bayfront house on Balboa Island for $10,000. I ridiculed him for trying to take me for a sucker. Maybe, just maybe, I should have listened to him. Earl saw the future a hell of a lot better than I did.

Black Bart

William Bartholomae may not have been the nicest man to ever live on Balboa Island, but he was far and away the cleanest.

Bill Bartholomae, or Black Bart, as he was sometimes called, was a fabulously rich oil man who became something of a character in Newport Beach yachting circles as a very stubborn man.

His most famous feat in the yachting world was when he piled his 140-foot yacht, the Paragon, onto the rocks of the west jetty during the big chubasco of September 20, 1939. When the tropical storm came roaring out of the Gulf of California, it came without warning. The Paragon was at sea with a party of sixteen. She had a very capable skipper. When the storm hit, Bart ordered his skipper to take the yacht into the harbor. There were thirty-foot waves breaking down the harbor mouth. The skipper told Bart the safest thing to do was wait outside, that the Paragon was quite capable of riding out the storm. Bart went into a rage, took the helm from the skipper, and tried to bring the vessel in. It didn't work. He piled the craft on the west jetty. It was a total wreck although the sixteen people aboard were saved. So much for Bart the yachtsman.

In addition to being pigheaded, stubborn and arbitrary, Bart had a passion for cleanliness. It was said that one could eat off the bottom of any of his oil rigs. He patrolled the oil fields constantly to see that none of his rigs had a drop of oil on them.

I was able to observe this fetish firsthand when Bart was living on Balboa Island. I think it was 1940 or 1941. He was living at 118 South Bay Front in a big, white, two-story frame house that is still there. It had a kind of funny wood siding. Bart had a Chinese houseman. He had that houseman wash down that siding every day with soap and water–the whole house! The houseman had some kind of special long brush that would reach all the way up the two-story sides of the house. I talked to the houseman once, and he told me that every day he had to unscrew the fronts of those wall gas furnaces we used to have and clean the back of the furnace. Something the rest of us did once a year Bart had done daily.

My sister lived next door to Bart one year, and on Sundays we used to watch as he brought his yacht into his dock and unloaded his guests. They weren't allowed to leave until they scrubbed down the yacht and the dock. It seemed to me that he didn't have too many repeat guests.
He finally built a huge mansion on the peninsula and moved off the Island.

Then he was murdered by his wife's sister. I don't remember many tears being shed over his passing. But he sure was clean.

The End Of Easter Week

It was Balboa Island that killed Easter Week.

For many years, Balboa had welcomed the onset of Easter vacation, not from any excess of piety but from the very crass point of view of money. Balboa lived off tourists who came in droves during the summer and spent enough money for the town to live on for the rest of the year. After Labor Day, Balboa went into hibernation. However, toward the end of that long sleep, the bear was getting a little hungry, and about the time Easter rolled around, the bear was famished. Easter Week provided some highly desirable sustenance.

I don't know how Easter Week in Balboa developed, but it was a living event when I arrived during the early Twenties. Hordes of kids from Southern California high schools and colleges would descend on the town, drink, play, raise hell and spend their money. They spent enough to carry the town until summer vacation. Balboa loved it. The kids couldn't hurt early Balboa with its single wall shacks and cottages unless they burned one down which, amazingly, never happened. Neither did the Balboans complain about a little noise. After all, noise made money.

Everything went along just fine until shortly after World War II. The town began to grow up. While we Balboans didn't know it yet, the honky-tonk era was coming to an end. Prohibition had been repealed, gambling was being outlawed, the Rendezvous burned down. Balboa was beginning to change. Still, Easter vacation, or Bal Week as it was now being called, continued, and Balboa grimly held on.

In the early Fifties, some new blood came into town. Mixed in that new blood was a group of enthusiastic, energetic young men who formed themselves into a new Junior Chamber of Commerce. The old one, the one of which I was the president, died with WWII when we all went into the service. Dean Bradford was the president of the new Junior Chamber, and among his faithful lieutenants were such notables in the history of the town as Moose Lagerlof, Ted Thomas, Ralph Hoyle, Joe Stamp and others.

Being ultra gung ho, they came up with a splendid idea. They decided to put on an Easter Week street dance for the kids, and they decided to put it on Balboa Island. By this time Balboa Island had grown from a scattering of houses to a full–even crowded–haven of year-round residents. A bedroom community, as it were.

The Junior Chamber cordoned off a block of Marine Avenue, hired a band, and put on a dance. It was a howling success–from the standpoint of the kids. They came in droves. They drank. They made noise. They surged up and down Marine Avenue and spilled over into some of the other streets. They had a great time.

But . . . instead of tolerating all these hijinks the way Balboa always had, the Balboa Islanders were outraged. What was good clean fun a couple of hundred yards across the bay was a real pain in the neck when it happened in your own front yard. They complained, they petitioned, they raised hell with the police department and the city council.

Based on their complaints and the complaints of others in this new non-resort community, the authorities finally clamped down on Easter vacation until it went away from this area entirely. It was Balboa Island that started it on its voyage to Palm Springs and the Colorado River.

And so we leave that crowded mud flat/marshy sandbar they now call Balboa Island and travel east to a flat place on the bluffs where cattle recently grazed, a place called Corona del Mar.

CORONA DEL MAR

Book Three

CORONA DEL MAR

With some reluctance I now let my daughter Nancy get into the act. She didn't know diddly about Balboa or Balboa Island. Since her mother didn't like Balboa, Nancy left that town while only a few weeks old. It is true that she spent some time on Balboa Island, but that wasn't of her choosing. Rather, she made it clear from the time she was a few months old that she wanted to go to Corona del Mar.

When we left Balboa we rented a house on the east bay-front of Balboa Island. Across the bay were some bluffs. And, invariably, outlined on top of those bluffs were horses. An Englishman named Mr. Harris had a stable nearby. His horses grazed at the top of that bluff. And horses, being vain animals, love to pose. And those stupid horses would stand there on the top of those bluffs day after day, posing.

And right across a narrow channel from those bluffs was a tiny girl named Nancy Gardner who loved horses. Before she could walk, she would crawl across the sand and into the water in an uncontrollable desire to get to those horses. Rescues were daily occurrences. Her father made a cage of chicken wire in which to keep her, to no avail. Her mother would look from the kitchen window while doing the breakfast dishes, and there would be her darling little daughter just disappearing under the water in her mad pursuit of those horses.

Finally, her parents surrendered, bought a lot and built a house in Corona del Mar, and there that little girl has lived, usually with a horse.

And so may I present my daughter, Nancy, the horse lover, who weaned me away from the water's edge and into the comparatively thin mountain air of Corona del Mar.

Nancy Gardner

Balboa Island wasn't a bad place to live. For a child there were sea walls to walk on, a place to get ice cream cones. The nice man at Hershey's Market always gave me a piece of bologna when we went in there. Still, Corona del Mar had it all over the Island. Even I, young as I was, could walk around the entire island in a relatively short time, but in Corona del Mar, civilization ended at the edge of town–in those days the boundary of what is now referred to by the rather precious Olde Corona del Mar–and beyond that the hills stretched on forever. There were gullies and ravines to be explored, vacant lots with shoulder-high weeds to play in, dirt alleys to gallop down, but the best thing about Corona del Mar, the thing that made it stand out over Balboa Island and every other part of Newport Beach, was that it had horses. But before we get to them, a little history from my father.

COPE BEN BOAT CO (Ben Cope) 817 State Highway
    Newport—758

Cope Ben (Sylvia) Ben Cope Boat Co h 721 Larkspur
    av Corona del Mar

Cope Margaret M (LA) 126 Ruby av Balboa Island

Copelin C M (LA) 215 41st st Newport

Corbin Claude G (Marie) r 308 Island av Balboa—537-W

Corbin Edwin H (Adelaide N) r 1204 E Central av Balboa

Cordeiro Manuel (Emily) smoked fish r 220 21st Newport

Cordeiro Saml (Juanita) fshmn r 1023 W Central Newpt

Corkum Annie B (Downey) 227 Diamond av Balboa Isl

Corneil Ethel Mrs r 628 W Surf Balboa

Cornelius H L (Fullerton) 128 25th st Newport

Cornell Fred h 327 Island av Balboa

Cornett W F Dr (Pasadena) 619 W Bay av Balboa

Cornwall Edwd A (Mildred) emp Std Oil r 220 Golden
    rod av Corona del Mar—386-W

Cornwell Ralph (LA) 307 Diamond av Balboa Island

Corona del Mar Bath House (John H Wernex) Bay Fr
    Corona del Mar—538

CORONA DEL MAR CAFE (Joe Rossi) 1611 State High-
    way Corona del Mar—phone 967

Coronado Apts (Mrs M L Wooden) 301 E Central Balboa

Coronell M S (LA) 302 Onyx av Balboa Island

Corrales N (LA) 120 28th st Newport

Corson Rex L (Margaret B) lather h 436 Fernleav C D M

Cort S A (LA) 131 E Bay av Balboa

Cortner Arthur F (Redlands) 900 Jasmine av Corona d M

Cottle's Grocery (H L Cottle) 2000 W Central Nwpt—606

Cottle H L (Regina) gro h 2000 W Central av Newport

Cottle Harris L Jr r 2000 W Central av Newport

Cotton Chas M (LA) 1509 E Bay Fr Balboa

Coulter Clifford chef Wilson's Cafe r 309 Palm st Balboa

Covert A T Dr (Long Bch) 128 36th st Newport—291

Covert Lawrence Wm (Carol) emp city h 506 14th Npt Hts

Cowen H H (LA) 127 Coral av Balboa Island

Cox Frances S Mrs h 1695 Pacific dr Corona del Mar

The History Of Early Corona del Mar

The early phases of history of an area are usually couched in the time-honored phrase, "lost in the mists of antiquity."

In the case of Corona del Mar, its early history is not lost in the mists of anything. Rather, its early history stands out in stark relief as having been born in the doldrums and remaining firmly encased in those doldrums for forty years. It took a world war to get the place out of those doldrums.

In 1904, James Irvine sold 700 acres of land behind Rocky Point to a man named George Hart for $150 an acre. It has been said that this was the only piece of the Irvine Ranch that Mr. Irvine ever sold. George Hart soon learned why.

Mr. Hart subdivided the land, put it on the market and began a vigorous sales promotion. Ten years later with only fifteen houses and a small hotel to show for his investment efforts he sold out and disappears from the history of Corona del Mar.

Balboa Island, under the promotional skills of W. S. Collins and his successors, had its ups and downs, its feasts and famines. Corona del Mar had only dreary failure. It continued to be a vast wasteland of vacant lots, most of them belonging to the City of Newport Beach, having been taken back from the original owners for nonpayment of taxes.

At one time, Frank Rinehart, the city clerk, acting on behalf of the city, offered every tax lot in Corona del Mar, hundreds of them, to Joe Rossi of Rossi's Cafe, for $10,000. Joe turned the offer down and never regretted his decision.

As late as World War II, lots were being offered for fifty dollars with no takers.

With that somewhat dreary background it is remarkable that Corona del Mar has developed into one of the more desirable living areas on the Pacific Coast–and it's hard to find any of those fifty dollar lots any more.

With that in-depth study of the early history of Corona del Mar, we shall now embark on a voyage of discovery–an effort to find out what happened to those fifty dollar lots.

The Discovery Of Corona del Mar

Part One: The Movie

My introduction to Corona del Mar was not nearly as damp as Nancy's numerous near drownings in her early struggle to get off Balboa Island and onto that bluff where all those horses stood. However, my introduction did have a damp aspect to it. Not for me but for an aspiring young motion picture actress.

In 1921 I came to Balboa from Wyoming at the ripe old age of ten to live with my older sister. After an early childhood of wandering the endless sagebrush plains of southwestern Wyoming, I found life on a narrow spit of sand between the ocean and bay somewhat restricting. Finally, my sister took pity on me. She gave me a dime for a ride on the launch that ran from the Pavilion in Balboa to the Palisades Hotel located in what we Balboans then called the Palisades. I understand that even then this area carried the legal name Corona del Mar, but we Balboans always called it the Palisades. By any name the place was ideal for running–700 acres of unsold lots plus the whole Irvine Ranch as a backup. An added incentive was that I might be able to see the home of Tony Deraga, who had already become a legend in Balboa for his numerous acts of heroism in saving foolhardy boatmen who dared the treacherous channel entrance only to overturn. Tony came to Balboa to pick up his mail, and it was one of my boyhood thrills to see my hero at the post office which was then located in the Pavilion. By going to Corona del Mar, I could see him in his native habitat as it were and might even see him dash down that long flight of stairs, leap into his dory and save someone.

All in all, the trip was a splendid idea on the part of my sister. However, something got in the way. That something was a movie in production.

As I jumped off the launch onto a float attached to a ramshackle pier at the foot of a long flight of steps that led to the Palisades Hotel, I discovered that a motion picture was being made on the float.

The scene that was being shot was one in which the heroine dived off the float, then came up smiling into the camera without a hair out of place just as Esther Williams was to do endless times about forty years later. There was one small drawback. Our heroine was no Olympic champion swimmer. Actually, she couldn't swim a stroke. She was scared to death of the water. This presented something of a problem to the director unless a solution was found. Another young woman, a swimmer, would dive off the float. The actress would then emerge from the water, smiling at the camera.

Finding an exact double was no problem. Each of the girls was wearing one of those awful bathing outfits of the era complete with bathing caps covered with gewgaws, a suit that came down to the wrists and knees, all festooned with lots of ribbons and frills, not to mention long stockings and rubber shoes. They were so covered up that Godzilla could have done the shot, and no one would have known the difference. The director selected one of the chorus who could swim and do the dive, and that part of the shoot was quickly handled. The problem came with getting a shot of the heroine coming up smiling.

To give an air of verisimilitude, it was decided that a large man would jump off the pier, making a suitable splash, then the heroine, who was submerged, would come to the surface with that smiling face. The water was only about five feet deep at this point, so the solution seemed perfect.

The man jumped and made the requisite splash, the camera recorded the splash, the director's assistant prodded the heroine who was crouched under water, she leaped up into the cameras smiling–except that she wasn't smiling. She was holding her nose, her eyes were squished shut, her hair was hanging down over her face, and she was spitting water with about the same velocity as a fire hydrant.

Take two. Three. Four. They did it again and again, each time with identical results, the eyes squished shut, the nose held, the hair down.

I spent all day on that float fascinated by the wonders of motion picture making. I became such a fixture that they let me hold one of the big reflecting boards that focus the sun on the object being photographed. I never left the float. I didn't walk up those stairs a single step. Finally, the operator of the launch told me that this was his last trip, so I left without ever seeing the Palisades or Corona del Mar, as some people called it.

And when I left, the heroine had still not completed the coming-up-smiling routine. I doubt that she ever did. I have a hunch that they wrote that sequence out of the script.

So much for my first effort to discover Corona del Mar. My next effort resulted in being thrown into a canyon filled with cactus.

Part 2–The Cactus Patch

Shortly after my abortive effort to discover Corona del Mar, my brother-in-law, Dick Whitson, with whom I lived, asked me if I wanted to ride over to the Palisades to see a movie company at work. Being an old hand at making movies by this time, I agreed to go. Dick was to deliver some box lunches to the movie crew. Getting to the Palisades was somewhat of a project. Of course, we could ride across the bay to Balboa Island on the ferry, but that cost fifty cents, and with Dick's Model T, one could drive forever on fifty cents worth of gasoline.

We filled the rumble seat with box lunches and started to the Palisades. First we drove up Newport Boulevard almost to Santa Ana, then along some dirt roads to the head of the upper bay. There we found a road that ran along the upper bay to where the present bridge crosses the bay. Here we turned and followed the present Bayside Drive to its intersection with Carnation. At that point the road ran up the side of the bluff, coming out at about Ocean Boulevard, then down Ocean Boulevard to Buck Gully. Today there is a road that zigzags down Buck Gully to Little Corona Beach. In those days we went straight over the side of the bluff and down the wall of the gully.

As far as the eye could see, Buck Gully was filled wall-to-wall with cactus. That was true of most canyons feeding into the ocean in those semi-arid days. Now, of course, all those canyons are filled with greenery, and the cactus is no more.

On Little Corona Beach, the movie company had erected an Alaskan fishing village. There were a couple of log cabins and a row of evergreens that had been stuck in the sand to block the view of all that cactus which would have looked a little odd in a picture about Alaska.

Because it was an Alaskan movie, it had Eskimos, or a lot of Mexican actors done up to look like Eskimos in heavy fur suits and boots, trying to take kayaks out through the surf and damned near drowning in the effort. I couldn't stay and watch the fun, though. Our job was to get down to the village with all those box lunches.

We drove to the edge of the gully. Dick set the brakes, and we began to slide down the side of the gully. A Model T has a high wheel base. About a third of the way down we hit a rock, and the Model T flipped. I went out on the first roll, but Dick rode it all the way to the bottom, turning over and spewing box lunches all through the cactus. Finally Dick was thrown out just before the Model T hit bottom. He landed in a patch of chollo cactus. When he stood up he had cactus sticking out of every part of his anatomy. I was lucky. I landed on my rear end on a piece of beavertail cactus.

The Model T landed right side up with the engine still running. Dick got in and drove it to the village. There a man with a pair of pliers spent quite a while pulling chollo spines out of Dick. The beavertail cactus attached to my rear end was easier to pry off.

Dick and I went back into all that cactus and retrieved the box lunches, and after watching the Mexicans try to take those kayaks out through the surf for a while we returned to Balboa. Thus ended my second effort to discover Corona del Mar.

My next effort came six years later and involved not a movie nor a cactus patch but a bathhouse.

Part 3–The Bathhouse

Six years after the cactus fiasco I had still not set foot on Corona del Mar although from the end of the peninsula one could almost throw a rock across the channel mouth and hit Rocky Point. While we didn't live on an is-land, we Balboans were certainly insular. We had everything a human being could want–liquor, gambling, two dance halls and, for the kids, limitless mud flats on which to play plus the best bodysurfing on the coast. Why leave Bal-boa?

By this time my brother-in-law Dick Whitson had become postmaster. One day I was hanging around the Pavilion, in which the post office was lo-cated, hoping to see my hero Tony Deraga appear to get his mail. On this day, Tony didn't appear, but a short, stocky man with a red face did, and after talk-ing to Dick made a gesture toward me. I advanced, and Dick said, "Bob, this is Captain Sheffield. He wants you to work at the Corona del Mar bathhouse this summer. It pays twenty-five dollars a month."

Wow! Double wow! Twenty-five dollars a month! I was working at the Green Dragon behind the counter washing glasses for ten cents an hour and not too many hours. Suddenly, I was rich beyond my wildest dreams. I ac-cepted, and thus made my third landing on Corona del Mar, as it were.

By this time Corona del Mar had become Corona del Mar, even to hard-ened Balboans. The name Palisades still stuck to the hotel which opened and closed with some regularity.

The old Corona del Mar bathhouse was located in what is now called Pirate's Cove. At that time there was a wide beach in front of the bathhouse which reached almost all the way across the bay to the Gillespie house and up to the Kerckhoff Laboratory on the Corona del Mar side. Those which are now bayfront lots in China Cove were then inside lots. Of course, all the lots were vacant. So were most of the lots in the rest of Corona del Mar.

The word "bathhouse" probably needs some explanation. Most beach towns had them, but they had nothing to with taking a bath–no pools, no steam rooms, no spas, no saunas, no Jacuzzis. They were simply places where people rented bathing suits for the day and afforded those people a place in which to change into those suits. At the Corona del Mar bathhouse we had three sizes–large, medium and small. They were ugly black, woolen, heavy Jantzens, men's and women's being identical except that the women had smaller armholes, I guess to keep their bosoms from falling out.

The bathhouse was erected on pilings and had two sections, men's and women's. Each customer had a small room in which to change from street clothes into those classy bathing suits. I soon discovered that I didn't really work for Captain Sheffield. Rather, I ran the bathhouse. He stayed upstairs in a little apartment built over the front of the bathhouse. There he drank. One day when he hadn't made an appearance for some time I climbed up on the roof and peeked in through a bathroom window. There was my employer stretched out on the floor. I assumed there was something wrong with him, and since I didn't have a key to the apartment, I broke a window in the bathroom to get in. When I did, I found out that he was simply passed out. When he came to he gave me hell for breaking the window and took the cost of repairs out of my salary. Incidentally, the "Captain" title he used came from having been a captain of the lifeguards at some English seaside resort. I never saw him near the water.

But who I did see was Duke Kahanamoku!

Hawaiian royalty, Olympic champion, he was in this country making movies. An avid surfer, he drove down the coast one day and saw the Corona del Mar surf, fell in love with it and began to surf there regularly. Soon he interested some of his more muscular movie cronies in the sport, and they formed a kind of informal Corona del Mar surfing club. They kept their surfboards in the bathhouse.

The Duke asked me to watch over their boards and see to it that no one stole them. Steal them? An average man couldn't even lift one. They were made of mahogany, twelve feet long, probably six inches thick, and must have weighed well over two hundred pounds. A few years later when I took up boardsurfing, my board was redwood and balsa, eleven feet long, and weighed a hundred and five pounds.

So I was watching over a bunch of boards that almost no one could lift or carry and by no stretch of the imagination was going to tote up that cliff out of the back of the bathhouse.

Nevertheless, the Duke asked me to watch over the boards. I did so, and in return, he would take me out for a ride on his shoulders. He was a powerful man, and I weighed less than a hundred pounds, so by what seemed no more than a flick of the wrist he had me on his shoulders and probably didn't even know I was there during the ride.

Years later during World War II, I met the Duke in Honolulu. I reminded him of the incident, and he claimed to remember me which I doubt seriously.

That year I drove to Corona del Mar seven days a week for the whole summer but never left the beach. I guess the rest of Corona del Mar wasn't very exciting.

Before I leave the Duke, I am aware that a couple of years previously he had saved seven men in the channel mouth. The launch Thelma overturned, spilling seventeen men into the water, and there was the Duke, Olympic gold medalist, Hawaiian royalty, movie star–by any normal standards his part in the rescue would be big news. But this was Balboa. We had our own heroes. We had Tony Deraga.

Antar "Tony" Deraga was a Russian-born meteorologist, hired in 1919 by the Orange County Harbor Commission to man a weather station on the cliffs overlooking the channel mouth at Corona del Mar.

While he did his meteorologist work and put up flags and warning devices and kept track of the sun and moon and tides and all that stuff that meteorologists do, the reason he became a legend was that he kept saving people from drowning in that same channel mouth. That channel mouth was very dangerous with no jetty at all one side and a decrepit one on the other. Nevertheless, people tried to go in and out of that channel mouth quite often, and equally often with disastrous results. Boats kept turning over and spilling their passengers into the water. When that happened, Tony would race down a long flight of steps from his meteorological station to a dory he kept at the foot of those steps. Then he would row out and save people, oodles of people. The local count was nothing short of astronomical, but even in reality it was nothing short of awesome, and if someone had said they saw Tony Deraga walking on water, it would have been accepted without question.

So when the Thelma overturned, what was the story? "Hey, did you hear? Tony Deraga and Charley Plummer saved five men today when the Thelma overturned in the channel mouth. Another guy saved some others. Five drowned. How about that Tony? He's something, isn't he?"

The Duke saves seven, and he's "another guy." As I say, Balboans. Balboans were insular.

Part 4–The Concrete Jetty

During the summer of 1927 when I worked at the Corona del Mar bathhouse, I noticed that a crew of men were making huge cement slabs on Main Beach. At the time I had not the slightest idea why they were doing so, but at the ripe old age of sixteen one doesn't go around asking adults why they are doing things.

I know now that in 1927 the concrete section of the east jetty was built, so that's what all those concrete slabs were for. The rock extension came much later.

I now realize as I walk my dog up and down the sidewalks of Corona del Mar that 1927 was also the year the Griffith Company was installing our sidewalks. All I have to do is look down at the sidewalks and there it is, "Installed 1927, The Griffith Company."

That concrete jetty was some engineer's aberration. It was an 800-foot sliver of concrete sticking out into the Pacific Ocean. It was built to help protect the harbor entrance. Instead it made the harbor entrance more dangerous. It had an amazing wave-making capacity. It could make small waves into large waves and large waves into monsters. It was a surfer's dream.

The boardsurfers–there were never too many of them–caught the waves off the end of the concrete jetty and, in those old heavy-board days–rode the shoulder into the bay. However, the bodysurfers stayed on the end of the jetty, then slid into the waves as they ran alongside the jetty and thus were able to take 800-foot rides to the shore end of the jetty. Of course, if you got too close to the jetty you lost a shoulder, but that was the chance you took. At the foot of the jetty was an iron chain ladder that one could climb, losing skin on fingers and toes, then run back on the upper lip of the jetty for another 800-foot

ride. It was such great bodysurfing that we loyal Balboa
beloved Balboa pier and trudge down to the Point, swim
all day at the Corona del Mar jetty.

We Balboans felt right at home on the beach at Co
Dirty George had transferred his hamburger operation
rona del Mar after being driven out of Balboa. He took
since Main Beach was so big the flies didn't seem to bother anyone. At Balb
with its narrow thirty-foot beach, Dirty George's flies drove us down to the
water's edge where it was cold and the flies would leave us alone. Thus, we
were glad to see Dirty George go. However, his way of doing business hadn't
changed with the locale. He still kept his hamburger patties in a big bucket of
water so they swelled up to enormous size. Then, when put on the grill, there
was a huge cloud of steam, and when the steam went away there was your
hamburger about the size of a silver dollar.

An interesting practice developed on that Corona del Mar concrete
jetty. The top of the jetty was always wet, and as a result, a kind of marine
moss grew on the jetty. It was slippery as ice, the same kind of slippery stuff
that one finds on the breakwater off the public beach at Waikiki.

With that slippery surface, a kind of primitive chicken game developed.
Two bodysurfers would run toward each other. Then they would throw themselves down on their bellies on this slick moss and slide toward each other. As
they approached, they would lift themselves on their fingertips and toes and
head toward each other on a collision course.

Theoretically, one would chicken out at the last second and drop to his
belly as the other slid over him. However, sometimes neither chickened, and
they would meet, two careening bodies, head to head.

The other possibility was that both would chicken. Both would drop
and they would still meet head to head but on their bellies. Same result, an

awful crashing of heads. Heads were bashed, necks were crunched, blood ran. Still, we Balboans would walk down to the Point, swim across and take part in this piece of idiocy.

Today, I have an arthritic neck that necessitates the sometime use of a neck brace. I attribute most of this to hitting my head on the sand bodysurfing for sixty years plus, but part of it is probably attributable to the Corona del Mar concrete jetty game of chicken. In addition, I undoubtedly sustained some brain damage which probably accounts for some of my more bizarre behavior throughout the years.

So much for my early voyages of discovery to Corona del Mar. In all candor I must admit that the place didn't loom very big in my thinking until, to save my daughter from drowning, we moved there.

The Stable

Nancy Gardner

I'm not sure that even then I believed that an entire family was relocated simply to placate a horse-mad five-year-old. Case in point: If the rest of the family was so solicitous of my passion, they would have bought me a horse. This did not happen. However, once we moved to Corona del Mar, I at least could abandon the wooden horse my grandfather had made me and take riding lessons on the real thing.

At the north end of town was a proper riding stable run by Lionel Harris, a silver-haired Englishman who lived on the bluff above the bay in a green cottage surrounded by eucalyptus trees. There was a large, airy barn with box stalls, a smaller barn for hay, a number of corrals, a riding ring, a pasture, flocks of ducks and geese and chickens–and all those horses. There were also dozens of little girls. Boys didn't seem to get the horse bug.

Mr. Harris, as he was always called, engendered the greatest respect from the children and grown-ups alike. Although reserved, as all good Englishmen are supposed to be, he was also very kind and patient, practically running a second home for the pack of horse-crazy girls who made up the main part of his customer base. His generosity may have had a self-serving edge since a dozen eager girls make a pretty good labor force. I could barely pick up my socks at home, and then only with a grumble, but at the stables I mucked out stalls, dragged bales of hay, whitewashed fences, soaped saddles and bridles . . . and begged to be allowed to do it the next day as well.

Mr. Harris owned a number of horses that he rented out for lessons, and the lessons were very thorough–the proper seat, the proper hands, the proper grooming of the horse afterwards–but the great goal of his students was to become proficient enough to join the Sunday ride. On Sundays he would mount his horse Dark Gem, a huge chestnut Thoroughbred nicknamed Jumbo, and lead twenty or thirty riders out of the stable yard, across the highway and up through a double row of tall eucalyptus trees that led to the reservoir. The eucalyptus were a beautiful sight as they curved up the hill, a landmark of the area, and I never imagined they would disappear. I didn't realize the ephemeral nature of landmarks in contrast to the desire to develop. Most of those trees were cut down for the Harbor View Hills development.

From the reservoir the ride headed out over the hills. The elite on their Thoroughbreds would break into a long gallop. The rest of us on our less-than-Thoroughbreds would trot, canter or–if we'd drawn an unusually good mount for that day–also gallop along unimpeded by streets, fences, anything but the time we wanted to spend. I saw my first bobcat on one of the rides, an occasional coyote, hawks, buzzards and snakes like the red racer that whipped through the dry grass. Our destination was an area called the Sheep Ranch, back of what is now Bonita Canyon but which then was little more than a couple of pens and a watering trough.

In the summer the ride occasionally went to Shark Island, a flat spit of sand, now Linda Isle, where we took the horses swimming. In either case, as soon as we got back, an army of girls set to grooming the animals and soaping all the tack.

In addition to renting horses, Mr. Harris also offered boarding for people who owned their own horses. Owning your own horse–somehow I couldn't make my parents understand the importance of this. Renting a horse was all right. It answered my need to ride, but I couldn't fall in love with a rental horse. What kind of romance was it when the very next week someone else was riding him? Each year as Christmas came, the same request was at the top of my list, and I spent Christmas Eve wondering just how my parents would be able to get my new horse into the living room. After all, the horse would be nervous . . . they weren't horse people . . . and if it had to go to the bathroom . . . but I needn't have worried since that was never one of my presents.

All I could do was envy the lucky souls who were owners. The actual owners themselves didn't make much of an impression. It was their animals I was interested in, and that's how I tended to identify the people–by the name of their horses. Mr. Red Fox, for example. A balding man with a potbelly. Mr. Red Fox was notorious because of his unfortunate habit of drinking and riding, only slightly less perilous than drinking and driving. More often than not horse and ride came home separately, Mr. Red Fox staggering in quite a lot later than the actual Red Fox, his gallant steed, and in much worse condition.

One boarder I did know by name, Joan Irvine, but not because of her association with most of the land around the area. She was noteworthy to me because she owned not one but two horses, an unbelievable bounty. It was my first indication that things weren't always distributed very equitably in this world.

Mr. Harris I respected and revered, but Katrina I idolized. She was a woman in her late teens or early twenties who lived with her mother in a second bungalow on the property. Many adults were intrigued by the possible relationship between the dashing Mr. Harris and his rather voluptuous aide, but since that was outside the world of horses it never even occurred to me to wonder. Katrina had long blonde hair, reputedly down to the ground, which she wore in braids coiled around her head, but that was the least of her attributes. She had her very own dog–something else I yearned for. Baba was a big black and white animal, about the size of a Great Dane, who guarded the stables, barking when anyone approached and keeping general order. Katrina also had her own horse, Relompico, which she could take over any jump. She could even crack a bullwhip over her head. In short, Katrina was everything to which a young woman could possibly aspire, and when I grew up, I was going to be Katrina.

From the time I was five until I was about ten she remained firmly ensconced on her pedestal. Then she left the stables for a period to go to this place called Europe. It was the first scratch in a heretofore impervious surface. I couldn't understand. Why would anyone in her right mind want to leave the stables, the most perfect place on earth? What could this Europe place possibly have to offer that wasn't at the stables?

After what seemed like a very long time, Katrina returned, but it was a changed Katrina. Katrina, owner of Baba the wonder dog, returned with this ridiculous frou frou poodle with bows in its hair, a dog that squealed if a chicken even looked at it. Worse, instead of rushing back into the saddle, she spent all her time driving around in this weird car, something called an MG, which didn't have room for a saddle or Baba or anything worthwhile. I was so disillusioned I left the stables shortly thereafter to take up my riding career at a new location. As for the stable, like the double row of eucalyptus trees, it became another victim of Corona del Mar's development. The buildings were razed to make way for Irvine Terrace, and Mr. Harris moved his operation to Fountain Valley.

The Pasture

Nancy Gardner

On a bright spring morning in 1953, Christin Neal, whose family owned Neal's Sporting Goods in Santa Ana; Ann Broering, whose father had started La Cantina Liquor Store; and I climbed down into Morning Canyon, at that time the end of Corona del Mar, and up the other side. As we galloped through the wild oats and mustard, imitating horses in a very excellent and true-to-life manner, we suddenly came upon the real thing which we promptly captured and led—or were led—to Al Beltran, a handsome Mexican-American who leased the three hundred acres on the ocean side of Coast Highway between Corona del Mar and Crystal Cove. Within an hour we had persuaded him to sell the horse, which had started the day with the service-able name of Pete but had since been rechristened the much more glamorous Ebony, and rushed home to persuade three sets of parents that without this horse we all surely would die. My parents, who had been immune to this argument so many times before, finally surrendered, and we ran back with sixty dollars, the agreed-upon price. That was the start of the pasture. For twelve dollars a month we grazed Ebony, nee Pete, and within a year there were a couple dozen horses grazing the pasture. Within two years, Al had a new business and could give up his former career of driving a school bus and running a few cows on the Irvine Ranch.

The horse establishments–Mr. Harris's and Al's–were at opposite ends of town and opposite ends of the emotional spectrum. It is tempting to say that the stable on the north end of town was cool Anglo-Saxon while the pasture at the south end was warm Latin American, but the differences may have been no more than an establishment run by a bachelor, Mr. Harris, and one by a family man who insisted everyone call him Al. Whatever the reason, things were much more informal at the pasture. There were no lessons, no rental horses, nothing but kids riding like Indians over all those acres. Instead of a man in jodphur pants and knee-high boots putting a jumper over a fence, there was a man in jeans and a battered cowboy hat on a wooden Mexican saddle twirling a lariat, and with every month the number of horses increased. One of the first increases was when we dissolved the three-way Ebony partnership, and each of us partners got a horse of our own. At last.

Before long, Al expanded into horse trading, driving up to Bob Kimbro's horse auction every few weeks. If he had a horse to sell, he'd try to take Julie Burns with him. Julie, the oldest of five Burns girls, was about three feet tall at the time. Most three-foot tall people find it extremely difficult to get on a horse. Not Julie. Agile as a monkey, she could scramble up the tallest horse much the way a rock climber scrambles up a cliff face. It was an amazing sight, and Al made the most of it. At the auction, Al's horse would be led out into the small ring surrounded by men with the blank faces of professional poker players. Bidding would start, a cursory process of nods and grunts and other quiet signals. Then Al would give Julie the signal. At the appearance of this tiny girl there was a confused mutter. She stood beside the horse which towered several feet above her, and then in a flash she shinnied up its side to the amazement and applause of the crowd–and the bidding skyrocketed. It was a sore disappointment–and money out of Al's pocket–when Julie hit puberty and started to grow.

Al also bought horses at the auction. Once he got them home, he'd throw on the Mexican saddle and put the horse through its paces. If it was sound and gentle he'd sell it to one of the local riders. If it wasn't sound or had a bad disposition he'd still sell it–but not to someone who was going to keep it at the pasture.

Whenever three or more kids get together they seem to form a club, and we were no exception. Within a year of the establishment of the pasture we formed the Centaurs. As part of our club activities, we put on horse shows including one for the parents in which a number of terrified mothers, mine included, clung desperately to their mounts as they hurtled around a ring to please their offspring, but the Centaurs' finest moment was our appearance in the Fish Fry Parade. Every year the Lions sponsored a parade as part of the Fish Fry, and as in any good parade, there were a number of equestrian groups that appeared. Seeing this, the idea quickly spread among Centaur members–oldest age thirteen–that we should participate. The club sent in its application, and the Lions Club, pleased that the parade would grow by the presence of one more prestigious riding group, accepted it.

The morning of the parade, thirty Centaurs rode their horses from Corona del Mar up to Costa Mesa where we proudly presented ourselves to the parade organizers. Unlike other equestrian groups, we had no silver-studded saddles. We didn't have any saddles at all. We also didn't have glittering matching outfits. We didn't have anything that suggested we were a group except for a hand-painted banner mounted on a broomstick. The parade organizers, to their lasting credit, didn't flick an eyelash but let the Centaurs ride in their parade, and when the people lining the parade route saw us–a motley bunch of kids in tennis shoes, tee shirts and jeans riding proudly bareback behind our home-made banner, they did the only thing possible–they applauded.

We went back the next year as well. By that time we had matching shirts, but we still didn't have any saddles.

The pasture continued to grow, even though a portion of the property was lost when Cameo Shores was built. With all those horses, the area became overgrazed, but makeshift corrals were erected, and the operation shifted to hay and alfalfa instead of free-range. Those of us who had been there at the beginning grew up and went off to college. Al finally lost the lease and opened a sandwich shop in Corona del Mar where Gary's Deli is today. New management came in and built stalls and a new ring, put up a proper sign, and a new generation of girls populated the place–and then that operation was closed to make way for Crystal Cove State Park, and now there's no place in Newport Beach for little girls to ride except for a remnant in Santa Ana Heights.

The Footbridge

Nancy Gardner

The Corona del Mar footbridge owes its existence to Frank Rinehart. He was city clerk and a very powerful politico. He lived on the peninsula, but his mother lived in Corona del Mar on Dahlia about a block from the ocean. Mrs. Rinehart, a lady no longer in the first flush of youth, didn't drive, so when she wanted groceries she had to hike the seven blocks to Marguerite, from there to the market, then back to Marguerite and the seven blocks home. While some might make the argument that this exercise kept the old lady rather spry, in Frank Rinehart's opinion it was too much to ask of his mother. The bridge was built to shorten her walk.

It may have been created as a time saver, but for me it was a life saver.

We moved to Corona del Mar, to a brand new, fire-engine red house at 235 Iris, just as I was to enter the first grade. A girl named Ruth Slater, prompted by her mother undoubtedly, had offered to walk me to school opening day, but there was some hesitation on my mother's part about letting me go. As she pointed out, I didn't know my way around yet. Until I did, wouldn't it be better if I just went to the corner and waited for the bus?

The bus? The baby bus with all the kindergartners? When I was a first grader? I turned to my father. Surely he had a solution. He thought a moment, then brightened. "You know your alphabet, don't you?"

Did I know my alphabet? I promptly broke into "ABCDEFG," singing the entire alphabet song while my father smiled dotingly. Such a prodigy. When I was finished with my bravura performance, he nodded his approval. "She won't get lost," he assured my mother. "All the streets in Corona del Mar are in alphabetical order," he told me. "If you ever don't know exactly where you are, just follow the alphabet."

Happy days. So there I was when Ruth arrived, with my new plaid dress, my new mary janes, and my new first-grade status, and off we started. It was a little confusing, up this street, down the next, nothing familiar, all of it new, but I tried to keep track. Left at the corner, down a couple of blocks, turn right and–wow! Right in front of us was this bridge spanning an immense canyon, a canyon so deep that when Ruth told me to look over the side of the bridge I nearly fainted. Then Ruth told in graphic terms what would happen to us if there was an earthquake at that moment. It was so terrible I had to close my eyes and run as fast as I could across the bridge before the earthquake hit, and as a result I didn't see much of our path once we left the bridge. In fact, I didn't see anything until we reached Corona del Mar Elementary School, between Carnation and Dahlia.

That at least was familiar since I'd gone to kindergarten there. There was the library, a tiny building across the playing fields from the school buildings where Mrs. Frazier reigned in gentle splendor. There were the rings I couldn't go around, the bars I couldn't make across. On friendly territory at last, I gave a jaunty wave to Ruth who was in the other first-grade class, and in I went.

What a change. No more sitting on the floor with our blankets. No more naps. None of that baby stuff. This was real school with tables and pencils and blackboards. This was the first grade, and I was so full of myself that I couldn't wait for recess to run out on the playground and chant, "Kindergarten baby, born in the gravy!" Just like the first graders had chanted at me the year before. So satisfying.

The hours passed swiftly, and soon school was out. Big first grader, I waited outside the classroom for my new friend Ruth to pick me up. I waited and waited, watching as the big yellow school buses pulled away, one after the other, and it wasn't until the last one left that I finally accepted the fact that Ruth wasn't going to show. So much for my new friend. More important, so much for my guide.

Now, a year before the solution would have been simple–burst into tears and cry until a teacher asked me what was wrong and fixed it. But I was a first grader. First graders didn't cry, even if their lower lips trembled woefully. First graders also knew their way home. I blinked back my tears and started off.

I got at least a half block before I was hopelessly lost. Had we passed that gray house? What about that yellow one? That row of bushes? I thought of going back to school, but I was too turned around to find it, so I walked. And walked. And walked. Then I walked some more. I wasn't supposed to talk to strangers, so there was no one to ask. There was nothing to do but walk block after block through an immense strange town, and I had just about accepted the fact that I would never see my parents again when . . . there it was! The first thing I'd recognized since I left the school–the footbridge. Even the threat of an earthquake couldn't stop me. Praying it would hold off a few more minutes, I darted across. Once safely on the other side I remembered the route, and a few minutes later I was strolling nonchalantly into the house.

Why had it been so hard? Why had I wandered around so haphazardly when my father had given me the key? Did I forget that the streets in Corona del Mar were in alphabetical order? No, I didn't forget. I remembered his words quite clearly. The problem was, although I could sing the alphabet, I couldn't read it. I would be wandering the streets of Corona del Mar to this day if I hadn't somehow stumbled upon the footbridge. I wasn't one to push my luck, however. For the rest of the year I rode the school bus.

Buffalo Bill And Mrs. Brookings

Nancy Gardner

One of the things I liked about Corona del Mar was that it seemed so wild after Balboa Island. Everything about Balboa Island was sedate. There were houses on every lot, a sea wall encircling the place, a gentle bay tapping at the sand. But Corona del Mar . . .

Huge waves crashed on the shore. Mountain lions lurked in the canyons. Cattle grazed on the hills, and people with shotguns hiked back in those hills and returned with dove and quail and pheasants. It was like living on the frontier. And we had our very own frontier hero. Buffalo Bill lived in Corona del Mar. I had seen him with my very own eyes which I reported that night at the dinner table.

My father not only took this with a large grain of salt, he flat out contradicted it. Buffalo Bill was dead, he told me, but I knew better. Buffalo Bill was alive and well and living in Corona del Mar, and the next day I dragged my disbelieving parent down to see him.

There he was, Buffalo Bill, standing in front of a long wooden building, his silver-blond hair cascading down his shoulders from under his broad-brimmed cowboy hat, an imperial drooping from his chin–just like every picture of Buffalo Bill I'd ever seen.

"See!" I said triumphantly.

Nothing daunted, my father approached Buffalo Bill who introduced himself not as Bill Cody but as Colonel Blake. I was suspicious at first. I'd seen enough movies to suspect he was using an alias, probably some Indian princess needed rescuing, but he agreed with my father that Buffalo Bill was dead, and finally I had to accept it. This wasn't Buffalo Bill, and with that I lost interest. I may have taken a cursory look at the Wild West collection he had inside the building, located on Coast Highway between Heliotrope and Goldenrod, but it didn't have that much on horses, and I soon lost interest. As a child, it never occurred to me to wonder how someone so enamored of that particular historical period ended up in a small beach town. I have queried others, but no one else seems to know either. One day Colonel Blake picked up and left town, and that was the last anyone heard of him.

Another establishment made a bigger impression. This was Brookings, Corona del Mar's own five-and-dime, run by a couple of the same name. Mrs. Brookings was a large, vigorous woman with strong features who had a brisk, almost martial air as she made her way down the sidewalk. Mr. Brooking was less imposing, a small, slightly stooped man with melting features who trotted behind his formidable wife a dutiful one pace to the rear, carrying her purse. In their store, Mrs. Brookings sat augustly behind the counter accepting payment with the gracious air of someone doing you a favor while Mr. Brooks scurried around helping customers find what they needed in the crowded aisles. The arrangement made a great deal of sense to me. I particularly liked the way Mrs. Brookings ordered her husband around; however, I have yet to meet my own Mr. Brookings who will accept such orders with such an amiable air.

Skin Diving

Newport, Balboa and Balboa Island had sand, lots of sand. What they didn't have was rocks. What Corona del Mar did have was rocks, lots of rocks. As a matter of fact, from Rocky Point to Ladder Rock, the waterfront is all rocks except for Main Beach and Little Corona.

Special mention should be made of Ladder Rock, the large arch rock off Cameo Shores. Referred to as Hollow Rock in early topographical maps, we locals call it Ladder Rock because for many years there was a ladder secured to the shore side of the rock. This was placed there sometime during the Twenties by my old boss Captain Sheffield, manager of the Corona del Mar bathhouse. The small arch rock, the one nearer Little Corona and just off Shorecliffs, is Arch Rock.

There seems to be some confusion between the two arch rocks. In one of the histories of early Newport Beach there is recounted an incident when a man named Tom Stark rowed a dory through Arch Rock on a day of big surf, and for that he received fifty dollars from the movie company for which he was acting as a stunt man rather than the usual twenty-five dollars for such a stunt. They must be talking about Ladder Rock. You couldn't put a kayak through Arch Rock on a still day. On the other hand, you could put a dory through Ladder Rock at high tide on a big day. I ought to know. Once, on a dare, I bodysurfed through Ladder Rock on a big day, an experience I will never, never attempt to repeat. Kids are crazy.

But back to skin diving. In 1935, Marco Anich went to Hawaii. There, being a superlative surfer, swimmer and all around waterman, he was accepted into a very clannish group–the Waikiki beach boys. Marco became thoroughly Polynesian. When he returned a couple of years later he brought a pair of bamboo underwater goggles used for skin diving. We tried them on and went absolutely crazy. Seeing the bottom of the ocean for the first time is a thrilling experience, and the bottom of the ocean from Little Corona to Ladder Rock was one of the most beautiful underwater gardens I have ever seen, and I have seen a lot of them around the world. You had the feeling you were the first human being to ever see what you were seeing. There were abalone on every rock, lobsters under every rock. There were millions of colorful fish, and most of them were so unused to man that they would literally swim up for a closer look as if to say, I wonder if this big hunk of meat is good to eat.

We tried to duplicate Marco's goggles without much success. Carving underwater goggles out of bamboo is an art. Then someone heard that at Fish Harbor on Terminal Island, a Japanese store was selling something called face plates (now called face masks). They were the answer to diving. I think they cost about three dollars.

When I see the modern scuba divers going in outfitted with literally thousands of dollars of equipment I laugh about our primitive outfit. This was before swim fins, so we couldn't buy them. Wet suits hadn't been invented, neither had snorkels, so there were two more items we saved on. Today, divers have elaborate spears that must cost a bundle. Ours were five-foot steel rods sharpened at one end. They didn't cost anything because Sam and Charley Oxarart, who worked at Douglas, smuggled out long steel rods by fitting them under their clothes between the armpit and the shoe. They must have had a somewhat awkward gait, but the guard at Douglas never caught them. We shot those steel rods through pieces of bamboo via heavy rubber bands. Ergo, our total outlay for diving was in the neighborhood of three dollars.

When we started diving, the ocean floor was virgin. A huge kelp bank stretched from Corona del Mar almost to San Diego. One dived under that kelp, swimming through the kelp forests, always keeping an eye out for a hole in the kelp surface, particularly at low tide. At low tide, the kelp compressed to about six feet of solid kelp which was almost impossible to get through on one's way to the surface. With the brown kelp, the green eel grass and that purple moss-like algae that grows on the rocks, it was one of the most beautiful sights in the world. And it all belonged to a handful of primitive divers.

Of course, scuba came along, and diving became popular. Man behaved in man's normal way. He destroyed everything with which he came into contact. He wiped out the fish population, the abalone, and most of the lobsters. The kelp went, and today, diving is a pretty sterile, unrewarding affair. But once upon a time, the diving from Little Corona to Ladder Rock was the greatest.

Speaking of diving, one quiet day lifeguard Bob Moore, later captain of the lifeguards, and I were the only two people at Little Corona.

Two men came down the hill. They were carrying a contraption that turned out to be a primitive diving bell. It was an old-fashioned hot water heater cut off to about a four-foot length. Holes had been cut in the side to fit over the diver's shoulders. A piece of glass had been inserted in the front for a window. A rubber hose ran from the top to an old-fashioned air compressor which operated much like the old-fashioned handcarts the railroads used.

Bob and I walked over to watch the operation. The men explained. One man would stay on the shore and pump air to the diver. That pumped air would hold the water line in the bell below the diver's head. Their logic was inescapable.

First the diver put on some deep sea diver's boots complete with lead weights. This, he explained, would hold him to the bottom. He then put the bell over his shoulders and began to shuffle toward the water. Those boots made walking very difficult. No doubt about it–they would hold him to the bottom. His friend began to pump.

Fascinated, Bob and I followed as the diver walked out into the water. Wading along beside him, we peered into the window. He smiled. As the diver walked out into deeper water, the water rose inside the bell. Checking back on shore we could see the man there pumping madly.

Water continued to rise inside the bell. Still the diver smiled. The water came to his chin. It came over his chin. Then it came to his nose. The diver began to look troubled. Instead of a smile there was a worried frown. The man on the beach pumped valiantly. The water still rose. Their theory was almost correct. The water did stop–just at the diver's eyes–and the diver was experiencing one of life's verities. One cannot breathe with both mouth and nose under water. His eyes kept opening and closing.

"He's drowning," I said.

"I know," said Bob, "but in all my years I've never seen a man drown right in front of my eyes. This is very interesting."

Duty won out over science, however, and Bob pushed the diver over, pulled him out of the bell, and the two of us managed to drag him up the beach despite those heavy boots.

After the guy gagged out some water, Bob told him and his buddy to take their diving bell home and practice in the bathtub.

They left, and we never saw them again. I don't know to this day whether they perfected their diving bell or drowned at some other beach.

Little Corona

Nancy Gardner

Little Corona wasn't just home to a few early skin divers. In the 1950s, Little Corona was the hangout of a wildly diverse group of bodysurfers, ranging in age from approximately ten to fifty and in occupation from artist to unemployed, united only by a love of the sun and sand and surf. This hardy group had a nominal leader, Eugene Scott, better known as Scotty, a tan, handsome man with graying locks. Scotty's professed occupation was home builder. Not developer. He'd build a house, sell it and live on the proceeds as long as he could. That was usually quite a long time because he had no trouble finding women, always gainfully employed, who seemed to take great pleasure in supporting him. Scotty could be found every day of the summer in his beach chair at Little Corona, always accompanied by his dog, McGroot. In those days, there were no laws against such a thing, or if there were, they were ignored. No one would have complained about McGroot anyway since he was a perfectly disciplined dog. Scotty pointed his finger at a spot, and that's where McGroot remained until Scotty told him otherwise. The only time I ever saw McGroot disobey was the time I brought our dog to the beach.

On the theory that one learns by example, I decided to bring Sam the beagle down to observe McGroot's impeccable behavior. It was a lesson he could stand to learn since not only was Sam not the highly trained animal Mc-Groot was, he wasn't trained at all–the only dog that in fourteen years never got housebroken. All that disobedience was now going to change.

I brought Sam down on the leash and had him observe McGroot lying obediently in his spot. After a sufficient amount of time had passed for the lesson to sink in, I let Sam off the leash and pointed to the spot Sam should occupy. I might as well have pointed at the sun. Freed of the leash, Sam did what every good beagle does and took off, sailing over bodies, kicking sand into eyes and mouths, knocking over small children, baying ecstatically and streaking back and forth over the beach with such mad abandon that McGroot finally succumbed and took off after him. Both Sam and I were sent from the beach in disgrace–once I captured him.

Like most groups, the Little Corona band had its rituals. As far as equipment, it was very simple–a swimsuit, an old sweatshirt (the older the better), a pair of Duckfeet fins and a towel. Scotty was allowed a beach chair because of his august position, but it would have been considered effete for anyone else. Towels were draped on the legs of the lifeguard tower, and everyone stretched out directly on the sand, usually in a circle, heads pointing to the center for conversation. From the bluff above it must have looked like a series of wagon wheels.

To go in the water, you picked up your fins and walked out waist-deep into the water where you put them on. To put them on in the sand and flip-flop to the water's edge was an unforgivable faux pas, labeling one as a tourist. There was nothing worse in the world. Upon coming back to shore, the progression was reversed. Fins were removed out in the water, you came in and took your towel from the guard stand, carefully dried your face, rehung the towel and flopped back on the sand again.

Little Corona

The reason the group congregated at Little Corona has often been debated. Certainly it didn't have the best waves in the area. The surf at Little Corona can best be described as short and sweet. On an average day, the usual ride lasts about three seconds. With any surf at all an immense rip develops, and on big days, the waves close out, making it more a matter of nerve than ability to take off. The reason for Little Corona's popularity was simple–we all lived in Corona del Mar. It was a lot easier to walk down to Little Corona than to ride your bike all the way over to Newport, or if you drove, to try to find a parking place over there.

There were lots of girls at the beach, but they were not part of the group. They were more a decorative feature. They sat on their towels or in their beach chairs and worked on their tans and never went in the water. The group of surfers was all male, with one exception–me. I always attributed my inclusion to the fact that I could surf with the best of them, but looking back at photos of me at the time I wonder. I was a late developer. Maybe with my skinny build they just thought I was another guy.

One of the problems of going to the beach every day, which we did, is that many days there was no surf which usually engendered some scintillating conversation:

"What crappy surf."

"For sure."

"It's terrible."

"You can say that again."

But after saying it again a number of times, you have to move on which we did, to playing cards while bitching:

"What crappy surf. Do you have any twos?"

"For sure. Go fish."

When we tired of that, there was always Cut the Cake. In this game, a small mountain of sand is built and a matchstick stuck in the top. Each player has to carve away part of the mountain, trying not to dislodge the match, a feat requiring great skill and dexterity.

After a really long, flat stretch, all those pastimes palled, and we developed the game known as V Rock. At the north end of Little Corona is Camel Rock, so named because it looks like the Great Sphinx. In other words, it looks nothing like a camel. It is a large rock, jutting about twenty feet above the sand. A lower shelf of rock extends from Camel Rock well out into the water, but where the shelf meets the Camel, there is a v-shaped notch, hence the name V Rock, much more truly descriptive than Camel Rock.

During one long, flat spell, a couple of the regulars meandered up the beach toward Camel Rock. A small wave came in, just a little soup until it hit V Rock where it compressed and shot up in the air. Bored minds as well as great ones tend to follow the same track. Within seconds the challenge was issued and a new game was created–V Rock. The rules of V Rock were simple. The player waded out through various submerged rocks that laced the area. Once at V Rock, he placed one hand on each side of the V and held on. When a wave came, it surged through the cleft and inundated him with foam.

The game was initially devised as a way to keep cool on hot days when the waves were too small to ride. However, there wasn't much competition in a game like that, so the stakes were raised. Now the challenge was to do V Rock when the surf was up. Now it was no longer a shower of white spray foaming through the cleft. Now it was a six-foot wall of water roaring through. If you held on, you won. If your grip slipped, you were tumbled into and over the surrounding rocks until you staggered back to the sand, bruised and bleeding. That was considered a loss.

The group at Little Corona lasted through the fifties. Then Scotty disappeared on some adventure. Real life in the sense of jobs and responsibilities took away some of the others. Sadly, on the cusp of the sixties, drugs took more than a few.

The other problem was that the beach began to disappear. At one time, Little Corona was a nice, deep sandy beach. The guard tower sat at the front of the beach on a wide swath of sand, and the beach itself was large enough for a volleyball court with plenty of space left over for sunbathers. But the beach began losing sand at an alarming rate. At least part of this was due to the small dam the city built across the mouth of Buck Gully, impeding the delivery of sand to the beach. As houses were built up along the canyon and inland, nuisance runoff turned a dry canyon into a wet one, and water now runs twenty-four hours a day down the canyon and across the sand, further narrowing the useful part of the beach. It's not a situation unique to Little Corona but one happening up and down the coast, one of the prices paid for development. It is sad to see what was once such a beautiful cove looking more and more like one of those rocky strands on the Riviera.

Griffith Etta h 810 S Bay Fr Bal Isl—640-J
Griffith J S (So Pasa) 1903 E Bay Fr Balboa
Griffith Lydia h 810 S Bay Fr Balboa Island—640-J
Griffith S M (LA) 939 Via Lido Soud Lido Isle
Grisswold May E (Covina) 125 Abalone av Balboa Island
Gronsky Roy (West LA) 2134 Miramar dr Balboa
Gross Herman O (LA) 3501 Finley av Newport
Grua Clipp P (San Marino) 1573 Miramar dr Balboa
Grua E T (So Pasa) 1521 Miramar dr Balboa
Grundy Gordon M (Nellie M) physician-surgeon ofc Newport Bch Hospital h 924 Ocean Fr Nwpt—25
Grupe A H (LA) 111 Grand Canal Balboa Island
Grupe Geo G h 237 Opal av Balboa Island
Gullatt W C "Bill" (Mary J) Pacific Yacht Repair h 1001 State Highway Newport—531
Gunderson D A (Georgia) mgr McCoy Drug r 107 A st Bal
Gunsolus Hattie B (Riverside) 108 8th st Balboa
Gunther M R O dogs r 1135 State Highway Newport
Gurley J A (Whittier) 1505 Miramar dr Balboa
Gurney Tom (LA) h 414 Fernleaf Corona del Mar
GUS' SEA SHELL CAFE (Gus Tamplis) 601 E Central av Balboa—555
GUS THE GARDENER 114 19th st Newport—510
Guthrie Jas V (Palm Springs) 813 W Bay av Balboa—358
Guyer Wm T r 1511 W Central av Newport

H

Haase Leo G (Hollywood) 609 W Central av Balboa
Haddock John E (Dorothy) road contr h 1740 Plaza del Norte Balboa
Hadley John W marine dock oper Beek r 208 Emerald av Balboa Island

Lifeguards

Today's lifeguard force is probably a lot more professional than in the past. Certainly the guards today are better swimmers. However, those early guards got the job done.

For several years, Don Vaughn was a lifeguard at Main Beach. Don was a large man–large enough to have played professional football. One day, a man was drunk and obnoxious on Main Beach. He was sitting on the sand at the water's edge next to the concrete jetty. The police were called. Now it is a matter of public knowledge that police hate to walk on the sand. So they asked Don to bring the man from the water's edge to the parking lot where the police unit was standing.

Don walked over to the drunk and told him the police wanted him. Too inebriated to properly appreciate Don's size, the drunk told Don to go to hell. Don repeated his request. The drunk looked up and finally took in all six feet seven inches of the man before him. "Carry me," he said with a smirk.

"No," said Don, "I won't carry you."

"How are you going to get me over there then?" the drunk inquired.

"I'm going to throw you over."

The drunk looked at the approximately two hundred yards of sand between him and the police unit. "You can't throw me that far."

"Oh, yes, I can," said Don. He picked up the drunk and threw him about eight feet. The drunk landed in the sand with a clattering of bones. Don walked over, picked him up and threw him another eight feet. This time the drunk looked at that two hundred yards of hard sand between them and the police unit and said, "You going to do this all the way over there?"

"Yes, I am, sir," Don smiled.

The drunk got up and staggered to the police unit.

One of the functions of a lifeguard is to provide information to beach visitors. One of the best at this was Wes Armand. He was assigned to Little Corona one summer. A man came up to him, pointed at the ocean and said, "How deep is it out there?"

At first I thought the guy was trying to be funny. Then I realized he was dead serious. He was from some place where people swam in rivers, creeks, ponds or lakes and always found out just how deep the water was before venturing in, particularly if they couldn't swim.

Wes could have been a smart aleck and pointed out that the depth went from a fraction of an inch at the water's edge to the Philippine Trench where it is miles deep, but instead he said gravely, "It's over your head, sir."

The man nodded and walked away satisfied.

I think that was one of the better answers to a question.

Phil Stubbs, who had been a longtime guard in San Clemente, transferred to Newport Beach where he was a lieutenant. That meant he got to drive a Jeep instead of sitting in a tower all day.

One day, Phil had brought the Jeep down to Little Corona, part of his route, and he and I were talking when a woman ran up to report that her little boy was stuck midway up the cliff.

We ran over and sure enough, a little boy was clinging to the side of the cliff about halfway up, screaming. He had just discovered one of the great truths about cliff climbing. It's a lot harder to climb down than up. He had come to an overhang and couldn't go either up or down.

Phil evaluated the situation. "If he lets go, he's a goner."

I agreed.

Phil said, "You go up and hang on to him, and I'll get the Jeep, drive to the top and come down on a rope and save him."

I looked at Phil who was about twenty-five years younger and considerably stronger. "Why don't you go up and hang on to him, and I'll drive the Jeep."

"Sorry, no can do. The Jeep is city property, and only a city employee can drive it."

It was hard to escape the logic of governmental bureaucracy, but I tried. "If I go up there and try to hang on to him and he let's go, both of us are going to come down, and we'll both be goners."

"True," said Phil as he got into the Jeep. "Don't let him let go."

The Jeep went up the hill, and I reluctantly went to the foot of the cliff and began to climb. Reaching the kid I told him to stop screaming, he was making his mother nervous. The kid did as he was told but confided that he was tired and couldn't hang on much longer. Remembering Phil's instructions, I said he had to hang on or both of us would go down. I tried to cover him with my body and prayed for Phil to hurry.

Phil drove to the top of the hill, put down the line and started down. A bunch of gravel came with him, and the kid began to scream again. I knew that any instant we were both going to crash down the cliff, but just as the kid let go Phil reached him. He grabbed him with one hand and with the other held on to the rope as they both slid down the cliff, leaving me poised gecko-like on its face. With much scraping and sliding and bumping and tearing I made it down to the bottom where the kid's mother was kissing Phil and whacking the kid. Me she ignored.

The next day there was a big headline story in the paper about how heroic Phil Stubbs had saved a kid from falling to his death from the cliff. I read the story carefully twice but could find no mention of my own part in the transaction.

When I inquired as to the omission of my name in the story Phil's answer was the essence of bureaucratic logic. "The lifeguard service needs the publicity. You don't."

Instead of rotating the guards on a daily basis, in those days a guard was assigned to one beach for the entire summer. There was a certain value in that. The regulars got to know the guard and all his idiosyncracies or even shortcomings. Bubba Broering, for example. Bubba was an excellent swimmer, a conscientious guard–and blind. Even with his thick glasses he could only see a few feet in front of his face and without them...

If there was any surf, the regulars became his eyes, keeping a sharp eye on the water at all times. Inevitably, a set would come through, mowing down any number of inexperienced tourists.

A yell would go up. "Bubba! Somebody's caught in the rip."

Like a retriever after a bird, Bubba was off. Grabbing his buoy he charged into the surf. With clean, powerful strokes he'd knife through the water, cutting the distance between himself and the floundering swimmer with each stroke–a hundred yards, fifty, ten. The swimmer's face lighted up–rescue was at hand–and Bubba would stroke right past him. You could see the victim madly swimming after Bubba, making futile grabs for the buoy in an effort to be saved. "To the right, Bubba!" someone would yell. He'd make the correction and eventually hook up with the swimmer. With a little help from his friends, he never lost one.

Another guard, Will Lippincott, presented a different approach. Some questioned whether Will even knew how to swim since nobody had ever seen him go in the water. Will seemed to regard his role as a guard as largely symbolic. On the roughest days he would recline in his guard tower, eyes half-closed, a bucolic smile on this face.

"Will!" someone would call. He'd look up lazily. "I think that guy's in trouble."

Will would look out to where some poor soul was flailing madly in an effort to stay afloat. "He looks okay to me."

The swimmer sank from sight, reappeared, sank, reappeared. "Will, it's his third time."

With a beleaguered sigh, Will would climb down from the tower, take his buoy and amble to water's edge where he would stop well short of the water. The swimmer, seeing the guard on his way, waved his arms frantically. Will would wave back, a companionable wave–not exactly what the swimmer was expecting. Fearing miscommunication, the swimmer would add yells for help to his waving arms. Will would nod and in a calm and reassuring manner beckon the swimmer as if he wanted to have a little conversation.

"Help!" the guy's screams and waves escalated. Clearly, the guard didn't understand what he was trying to tell him. Will on shore smiled and waved back and again signaled the swimmer, like the end of a game of hide and seek. "Allee allee outs in, free free free!"

That's exactly what the swimmer wanted–to come in–but he couldn't. He was inept, inexperienced and on top of that, panicked.

A couple of surfers on the beach would gather their fins, ready to make the rescue, but Will would calmly shrug them off, and so we sat there on the sand, holding our breaths, waiting as the swimmer went down for the last time. But for some reason, the swimmer never went down. After all the waving and all the shouting, he finally got the idea that this weird lifeguard on the beach was not coming out in the water. Bobbing, flailing, buffeted by the surf and spending as much time under as on top of the water, the swimmer would set out, floating closer and closer to shore until he finally crawled up on the sand under his own power. Satisfied with another successful rescue, Will would return to the tower, not even his toes wet. It was an amazing performance, and the only explanation anybody could come up with was that Will's laid-back attitude somehow imbued the swimmer with unfounded but useful confidence. Seeing Will's stoic refusal to rescue, the swimmer must have thought, "That guy's a lifeguard, and he doesn't seem to think I'm in trouble. I guess I'm not." And that was enough to see him in.

Nancy Gardner

If Will had a laissez fair attitude toward life saving, Jim Adams's philosophy seemed to be, "If it moves, rescue it." Jim had all the earnestness and most of the size of a St. Bernard. He was there to rescue people, and, by God, he was going to rescue them. Many people were dragged in kicking and screaming, not because they were in distress but because they hadn't needed rescuing.

If you didn't want to be saved, you had to keep up a good show at all times which meant most people spent their time in between waves swimming laps, just to show they weren't in trouble. Wave to a friend, and Jim was instantly at your side, thrusting his float at you.

"But Jim," you would protest, "I'm not in trouble."

"Don't be embarrassed," he would say, draping you around the buoy, "Everyone needs help at one time or another."

"But not now, Jim. There's a set coming."

But he could never be prevailed upon to cease and desist, and the best thing was just to submit to the ignominy of being towed in to shore, fill out the report with as little irony as possible, and swim back out, being very careful not to signal to anyone the next time.

If it hadn't been for his ardent sincerity, Jim might have been hated by his constituents, but as he was completely unbiased and rescued everyone regardless of race, color or need, he was accepted as part of the Little Corona culture.

Babbitt Lillian M (Pasa) 309 Apolena av Balboa Island
Bachman Leo (Louise) Bachman Service Station r 3090
    W Central av Newport
BACHMAN SERVICE STATION (Leo Bachman) 3090
    W Central av Newport—765
Bachmann Arthur M (Meta) h 208 Ruby av Bal Isl--700-J
Bachmann Clara (LA) 208 Ruby av Balboa Island
Bacon Delight G (LA) 609 N Bay Fr Balboa Island
Bacon Geo Mrs (San Marino) 120 Sapphire av Balboa Isl
Bagley H K (So Pasa) 106 Apolena av Balboa Island
Baker Blanche Mrs r 617 Heliotrope av Corona del Mar
Baker C W (LA) 332 Buena Vista blvd Balboa
Baker Frank (Riverside) 112 26th st Newport
Baker Geo H (Louise) h 2144 Ocean blvd Balboa
Baker Grace M (Pasa) 2057 Ocean blvd Balboa
Baker Harry S (Etta) El Bayo Service Station r 1439
    W Central av Newport
Baker Howell Mrs (LA) 802 S Bay Fr Balboa Isl—270
Baker Howard E (Pasa) 515 Acacia av Corona del Mar
Baker Jack W (LA) 201 Topaz av Balboa Island
Baker Minnie Mrs r 318 Lindo av Balboa
Bakeman Mollie (Fresno) 1301 N Bay Fr Balboa Island
Balaton's Cabins (P G Balaton) 6504 State Hiway Newpt
Balaton P G (Ethel) serv sta & Cabins r 6502 State Hiway
BALBOA APTS (T W Heath mgr) 303½ Main st Balboa
Balboa Beach Amusement Co (Rendezvous) R G Bur-
    lingame pres 600 E Surf Balboa
Balboa Candy Kitchen (I Weiner) 400 Main st Balboa
BALBOA CANVAS SHOP (H P "Omar" Norman) 224½
    21st st Newport—207
BALBOA FURNITURE CO (John F Vogel) 304 Main
    st Balboa—145-W
Balboa Hotel 204 Main st Balboa
Balboa Inn (V A Kirschler) 105 Main st Balboa—660
Balboa Inn Restaurant (C E Dickens) 716 E Surf Balboa
Balboa Island Ferry Line (J A Beek) ofc 410 S Bay Fr
    Balboa Island—62-W
Balboa Island School of Swimming & Diving 611 N Bay
    Fr Balboa Island

Politics And Politicians

The political history of Corona del Mar, like Caesar's Gaul–and Balboa Island–is divided into three parts. Part One: Nothing. Part Two: Red Hill. Part Three: Outstanding community leadership.

Part One covers the period from the beginning of time to 1923 when Corona del Mar was annexed to the City of Newport Beach. During that period, the city and its politicians had no interest in Corona del Mar. Since it was not part of the city its inhabitants, few though they might have been, couldn't vote in city elections, and in politics, if you can't vote, you don't exist. Corona del Mar was of no more interest than Tustin, politically speaking.

Part Two I have labeled Red Hill. This period covers the time from the annexation of the city to World War II. Although Corona del Mar was now part of the city, politically speaking it was something of a mystery to the rest of the town. It didn't fit into any handy little political groove.

Shortly after the annexation of Corona del Mar, there was a political revolution in the City of Newport Beach. The Newport group that had run the city since its incorporation was ousted by a group of young Balboans led by a man named Lloyd Claire. From then until WWII, Lloyd Claire was, to all intents and purposes, the political boss of Newport Beach.

I do not mean to bad-mouth the Claire administration. After all, it dragged the city through the Great Depression when other cities were going belly-up. It kept the harbor from becoming a commercial port like San Pedro. It was during the Claire administration that the dredging of the bay took place, an event most historians cite as the number one reason for the growth of the City of Newport Beach to its present position as the most desirable place on the Pacific coast in which to live. But the Claire administration was machine politics. A small group of men from one part of town ran the whole city. Granted, they did much for the city. Nevertheless, a dictatorship is still a dictatorship, even if it is a benevolent dictatorship.

It was during this part of the political history of the city that Corona del Mar acquired the nickname of Red Hill.

The rest of the city could be trusted to vote solidly for the administration and its program of growth, progress, development, expansion and any similar catchwords or phrases, but Corona del Mar?

Just before a municipal election, Lloyd Claire would call together at the old city hall all the faithful, the administration and its loyal supporters. Lloyd would go through each precinct name by name, assigning someone to contact each and every voter to see to it that that voter would vote for the administration's handpicked candidates. At each name, someone would nod. Yes, that person would be voting for the administration.

Everything would go along as smooth as clockwork until the Corona del Mar precinct came up. At that point all eyes turned to Johnny Siegel, assistant city engineer. He lived in Corona del Mar which made him the administration's unofficial contact in that area. When a Corona del Mar name was called, instead of a perfunctory nod, Johnny would shake his head, purse his lips and in an embarrassed way confess that he couldn't absolutely guarantee how that individual was going to vote.

Perhaps it was the mountain air of Corona del Mar as contrasted with the sea-level air of the rest of the city. Whatever the cause, Corona del Mar seemed to be full of people who declined to march lockstep with the rest of the town. It was disturbing. Worse. It was subversive. Hence the nickname Red Hill.

To add fuel to the fire, it was rumored that there were even some *Democrats* in Corona del Mar. That suspicion became a certainty a few years later when Chuck and Dee Dee Masters came to town and announced that not only were they Democrats but even more shocking, they were *liberal* Democrats!– and not ashamed of it. Red Hill, indeed!

Now to Part Three of the political history of Corona del Mar. Came WWII and the end of the Lloyd Claire administration. A new breed came into power in City Hall, young, enthusiastic, high-principled men of honesty, intelligence and integrity who helped the city outgrow machine politics. Among this group were two outstanding men from Corona del Mar, Braden Finch and Clyan Hall, and they were followed by the likes of Jay Stoddard, Andy Smith, Hans Lorenz, O.Z. Robertson, Les Steffensen and, more recently, Phil Sansone.

Sometime during the early fifties I appointed Braden Finch to the position of chairman of the Orange County Grand Jury.

At that time, the five supervisors ran the county down to the slightest detail. Actually, the county was operated as five separate fiefdoms. If you had a problem in the First District, no matter how small, you went to Cy Featherly, supervisor from that district. The same was true of each of the other four districts, and these men who were micromanaging the county had only one qualification for their jobs. They had received more votes than their opponents. Then along came Braden Finch.

When his Grand Jury filed its final report, rather than concluding with the usual platitudes about how well the county was getting along under its five supervisors, Braden's report branded the whole arrangement as a "horse and buggy" way of running the county. He suggested that the county hire a manager, an experienced, capable person educated in the field of public administration, to run the county, leaving the supervisors to handle matters of policy. The supervisors were annoyed, but the public reaction to Braden's report was such that they had to do something. They did. They hired what they called a county administrator, but they never gave him the power to be a real county manager, a CEO, as it were.

Had the county followed Braden Finch's recommendation made some forty years ago, the county might well not have experienced a certain unpleasantness that happened to it in 1995.

The Watchdogs

Every city needs its watchdogs. Most of us sit on our rear ends and leave the direction and decisions to our elective and appointive public servants. And most of the time that happy arrangement works, lazy though it may be. This is because most of our elective and appointive public officials are honest, hard-working dedicated public servants. But not always. It is then that our watchdogs become important. And Corona del Mar had two of the best in Mary Burton and Izzy Pease.

At one time, the time of Ma Fisher and Mrs. Maxwell and Lancey Sherman, we had to worry about the problems inherent in the unhealthy influence on the city of liquor and gambling. However, in spite of ourselves we outgrew the honky-tonk era and embarked on a new and exciting program—development and expansion. It was then that watchdogs interested in protecting the environment and our way of life became important. And, as I say, Corona del Mar had two of the best.

We begin with Mary Burton who came to our town as a child in 1909 and has lived to this day in one of those wonderful redwood houses overlooking Main Beach. And because of Mary Burton we have that Main Beach.

Main Beach was at one time owned by the Citizens Bank of Los Angeles, which also owned China Cove and the old Corona del Mar bathhouse at which I once worked. Sand doesn't generate much income, so all of China Cove was laid out in nice residential lots. One of the most beautiful natural coves on the coast was transformed into a very desirable residential area, and Main Beach was headed for the same fate.

Like China Cove, it was laid out in nice residential lots by the bank. When a question was raised as to the appropriateness of this, the city attorney issued an opinion: That area was zoned for residential use, and there was nothing the city or anybody else could do about it. Everybody, including the city council, meekly accepted his position–everybody but Mary Burton. She thought the beach should remain a beach, and she couldn't believe there wasn't something that could be done to protect it. She nosed around, refusing to be discouraged, and her persistence finally paid off. It seemed that the city attorney had a slight conflict of interest. He not only represented the city, but he also represented the bank. When she revealed this, the city attorney disappeared, the city went along with the state's plans for a public beach, and the present state beach exists, thanks to Mary Burton. Without her one would look down from the bluff and instead of seeing one of the most beautiful beaches on the coast, one would see houses jammed together a la Surfside in Seal Beach.

In her effort to save Main Beach, Mary Burton had the enthusiastic support of Izzy Pease. Izzy's full name was Isobel Andrews Pease, but no one ever called her anything but Izzy. She took part in all of the programs aimed at informing the public of environmental problems facing the city, but her own particular program is the one I will always remember.

To me, Izzy Pease was the Johnny Appleseed of Corona del Mar. You remember Johnny Appleseed, the man who ranged the Midwest in the early days planting apple seeds from which apple trees sprouted. While Johnny and

Izzy never met, they should have. They were kindred spirits.

In the early days, Corona del Mar was pretty bleak, just a flat place with some lonesome roads. No trees, no shrubbery, not quite the Gobi Desert but close. Izzy Pease decided to do something about it. I remember when I built my first house in Corona del Mar, Izzy was there as soon as the contract was let asking me what kind of trees I was going to plant. Every newcomer got the same treatment, and Izzy wasn't one to be brushed off lightly. She was willing to use whatever weapons were at hand to achieve her goal of more trees.

One man, who shall go unnamed, was building a house in Corona del Mar. Izzy arrived one morning and in her brisk manner demanded to know what kind of trees he was going to plant. He was a grouchy guy who didn't take kindly to a rather chunky woman with bright blue eyes telling him what to do. He told her so.

The blue eyes became steely. "You better plant some trees," she warned him.

He told her to shove off.

That night there was quite a severe earthquake, and first thing in the morning Izzy was back at this house. "See what happens when you try to fight me?" she said.

The man surrendered and planted a tree, and now many streets of Corona del Mar are noted for their trees.

Tetzlaff Selma Mrs h 310 El Modena av Newport Heights
Tetzlaff Ted (Hollywood) 409 Edgewater pt Balboa
Texaco Marine Dock (Wm H McIntee) 2406 W Central &
    Bay Fr Newport
Texaco Service Station (W H McIntee) 2406 W Central Npt
Thayer E W (LA) 1222 E Central av Balboa
Thee Lois E Mrs (LA) 205 Crystal av Balboa Island
Thibodo F E (Drainge Constn Co) ofc 2616 W Central Npt
Thomas Clarke R (Vivian) r 111 Crystal av Balboa Island
Thomas F' C (Upland) 123 E Bay av Balboa
Thomas Helen L h 3314 Ocean Fr Newport
Thomas Hepton L (Berta) Mermaid Malt Shop r 2205½
    Coast blvd Newport
Thomas J A (LA) 301 E Bay Fr Balboa Island
Thomas Jack (Mabel) Bayview dr & Goldenrod av C D M
Thomas J H (LA) 111 Diamond av Balboa Island
Thomas J O (San Marino) 306 Sapphire av Balboa Island
Thomas L A (Long Bch) 1518 Ocean Fr Newport
Thomas Roy E Dr (Georgia) 28 Harbor Island
Thompson A S (Julia M) Red & White gro r 112 24th Npt
Thompson & Bowman (Roland Thompson—Frank L Bow-
    man) attys ofc Storey Bldg Balboa—224
Thompson Clayton (Gladys) area-slsmn Standard Oil
    r 310 Anade av Balboa
Thompson Emma C Mrs h 900 E Surf Balboa
Thompson F L (LA) 200 Diamond av Balboa Island
Thompson Harold S (Mimmie) Nabrhd Gro r 200 30th Npt
Thompson Herbert A (Alma) Red & White Store r 127
    43rd st Newport
Thompson Leonard tchr High Schl r 1727 Ocean blvd Bal
Thompson L H (Glendale) 204 Abalone av Balboa Island
Thompson L K (Gelndale) 1600 Balboa av Balboa Island
Thompson Mary Mrs (Pasa) 720 W Central av Balboa
Thompson's Market Red & White Store (A S & H A
    Thompson 112 McFadden pl Newport—415
Thompson Roland (Ruby) city atty h 1011 W Central av
    Newport—1916

Corona del Mar's Restaurant Row

Newport Beach has reason to be proud of its very distinctive restaurant row, stretching as it does along Mariners Mile from the Arches to the Bay Club. I am not aware of any other place on earth that can boast such a row of first-class waterfront restaurants packed so close together that one can literally step from one fine restaurant to the next. At one time, Pete Siracusa even built one of his Ancient Mariners right next door to one of his Rusty Pelicans. Now that's restaurant chutzpah.

However, Corona del Mar had its own restaurant row while that stretch along Mariners Mile was nothing but a long stretch of bare sand with a few ramshackle boatworks to break the monotony.

While Balboa had more than its share of bars, it could only claim two restaurants of style, Christian's Hut and The Doll House.

All Newport had was the Arches.

Balboa Island had to struggle along with the Park Avenue Cafe. While its bar housed a colorful cast of characters, the Park Avenue was never known as an outstanding eating place.

Ah, but Corona del Mar . . .

THE HURLEY BELL ~ TAIL OF THE COCK

At the east end of the Pacific Coast Highway in Corona del Mar stands a Tudor-style mansion draped in ivy. Two very proper English ladies, Marguerite McCullock and her mother, built the place which is an exact replica of a famous inn in England, the Hurley Bell.

Originally it was to be their home, but they soon realized its commercial potential and leased it to a series of fine restaurant operators.

The first restaurant in the Hurley Bell building was the Tail of the Cock which operated during the late thirties and early forties. The original Tail of the Cock was a pipe dream of two self-styled ham actors who started a restaurant in Los Angeles that became an instant success. They branched out and opened a second Tail of the Cock in the Hurley Bell building. When they broke up, one of the partners, Bruce Warren, took over the Corona del Mar operation. It was also an instant success, with food, service and ambience just as good as the Los Angeles operation. I think it was probably the first real uptown restaurant in the City of Newport Beach. Bruce Warren may have been a ham actor, but he brought real talent to the restaurant business. It was a class operation. It was also the hangout of a struggling young lawyer named Bob Gardner.

Bruce Warren became my client. He had more legal problems than that legendary dog has fleas. We had one small problem. While Bruce was a fine client insofar as churning legal business, he was always a trifle short of cash. So we worked out a deal. I would take care of all of Bruce's legal problems, and in exchange I would have an open-end account at his restaurant. It was a gamble for each of us. I had to make enough money outside Warren's account to pay my overhead, and he had to serve enough other customers to carry me. However, it worked out just fine, and neither of us ever complained about the arrangement.

Of course, with an open account at the best restaurant in town I became the last of the big spenders, Diamond Jim Brady himself. And so it was that one night I was wining and dining a young lady in the Tail of the Cock when a very dramatic incident took place.

Tiny Vaughn was the constable of Newport Beach Township. This was before municipal courts and municipal court marshals. Our local justice of the peace was Donald Dodge, and Tiny Vaughn was his constable.

Tiny's actual name was Frank, but I never heard anyone call him by that name. Tiny wasn't tiny. At six foot seven he was a huge slab of a man who must have weighed well over three hundred pounds. His son, Don, was also six foot seven, but he was practically skinny compared to his father. Picture three fifty-gallon oil drums placed on top of one another. That was Tiny Vaughn.

Theoretically, the constable limited himself to serving papers. At least that was what Constable Big Bill Ponting, Tiny's predecessor, had done. Not Tiny. Tiny had been a cop and believed in enforcing the law in his township. The township included Newport Beach and what is now Costa Mesa. After a couple of head-to-heads with Rowland Hodgkinson, chief of police of Newport Beach and a pretty tough guy himself, Tiny stayed out of Newport Beach. However, Costa Mesa became his fiefdom. It was then unincorporated, and the sheriff simply surrendered to Tiny who took over all law enforcement there.

Some of his efforts were a trifle irregular but highly effective. For example, a certain bar had a bad reputation for serving drunks. Tiny didn't waste any time remonstrating with the management. He just parked his big Buick outside the bar and arrested every drunk that staggered out. The bar owner complained to the Grand Jury, but the Grand Jury said, in substance, "Go get 'em, Tiny." The owner of the bar quit serving drunks.

But back to the Tail of the Cock. Many people didn't know that Tiny Vaughn had an artificial leg, replacing one lost in a traffic accident. With that artificial leg Tiny had a pretty good parlor trick. Given the right occasion he would whip out his pocket knife and bury the blade to its hilt in his leg. For someone who didn't know it was an artificial leg, watching this was an unnerving experience.

And so it was that on this particular night while I was wining and dining the young lady at the Tail of the Cock, Tiny Vaughn and Marcus McCallen were sitting at the bar. Marcus McCallen was a wealthy Huntington Beach oil man and was at that time mayor of Huntington Beach. He was also very much a part of the saloon culture of the City of Newport Beach–always putting a hundred dollar bill on the bar and leaving it there until everyone in the house had drunk up.

I noticed Marcus looking over his shoulder at me and my date, then whispering something to Tiny. With that Tiny roared in a voice that could be heard in Laguna, "That's right, Mac!" At the same time, with every eye in the place on him, he pulled out his knife and buried it to the hilt in his leg.

Plop. My date fainted right into her salad.

Marcus looked over his shoulder and said with his well known stammer, "B-B-Bob, she's not for you. She d-d-doesn't have what it takes."

He was right, of course. She didn't have what it t-t-took. I don't know what she would have done had she been in the Glider Inn in Seal Beach the night Tiny pulled out his trusty .45 and blasted a hole in the bass drum while the drummer was still playing. Something about not keeping the beat. It took a certain stamina to be around Tiny Vaughn. My date didn't have it.

World War II wiped out Bruce Warren due to the wartime blackout. The lack of traffic on Coast Highway was the end of the Corona del Mar Tail of the Cock.

After the demise of the Tail of the Cock, Fred Hershon ran the place and ran it as the Hurley Bell. Fred's was another class operation, what may well have been up until that time the best restaurant in the history of the City of Newport Beach.

While the restaurant was ostensibly operated by Fred, not a dish left the kitchen without undergoing careful inspection by his wife, Mildred. The food at the Hurley Bell was superlative.

After Fred Hershon left, the Hurley Bell operated under a variety of ownerships with varying degrees of success or failure until 1965 when the Five Crowns took it over. It has been operating a very, very successful restaurant on the Hurley Bell site since then.

THE DRIFT ROOM

Across the street from the Hurley Bell and west toward Marguerite was the Drift Room operated by "Monte" Montgomery and his wife, Reba. While not in the same class with the Tail of the Cock or the Hurley Bell, the Drift Room could hold up its head with any modern-day restaurant. More important, the Drift Room was a favorite bar of Sam Oxarart.

Sam Oxarart was a character. A thoroughly delightful man, warm, friendly, decent, Sam seemed to march to a different drummer than the rest of the world. Peculiar things happened to Sam.

And so it was that Sam was drinking in the Drift Room. Having had a few and being a good citizen, he asked Monte to call a taxi for him. Monte did and said the cab would be by in a few minutes and would pick Sam up in the alley.

In a few minutes Sam went out the back door, and sure enough, there was a car waiting. He hopped in, told the driver his address in Shorecliffs, and sat back to enjoy the ride to his home. As he did so, he looked out the window and saw an odd-looking thing on the left front fender of the car.

"Driver, what's that thing on your front fender?"

"The siren," said the driver.

"The siren?" said Sam.

"The siren," repeated the driver, turning his head.

Sam stared at him a moment. "This isn't a taxi, is it?"

"Nope."

"Well, I seem to have made a slight mistake."

"That's all right," said the good-natured police officer. "I'll take you home."

He did. There he had a terrible time getting rid of Sam. Sam wanted him to come in for a drink and was quite insistent. Finally the policeman managed to get rid of his passenger and drove away, wondering whether to report the incident to his superiors. He didn't, which was just as well. Some senior police officers would take a dim view of such a humanitarian approach.

PAPA GINO ~ THE CHEF'S INN ~ CHAOS

At the corner of Coast Highway and Marguerite stands a building that has had a remarkable page in the history of Corona del Mar.

First it was a bakery operated by Papa Gino Borero, father of future restaurant great Gino Borero. Papa Gino owned that whole corner. He built a modest bakery, then made it into a beer joint with big-busted gals serving the beer. Then Robert Hill came along. Bob Hill was a successful restaurant operator from Pasadena. He secured a lease on the property from Papa Gino, tore down the bakery/beer joint, and built the Chef's Inn.

Bob Hill built the place, but then he turned the operation of the restaurant over to his daughter Claudia "Coy" Hutson and her husband, Hugh. They turned it into the most popular watering hole in town. Not only did it have outstanding food, it had a very, very popular bar featuring a superlative piano player named Mel, whose last name I've forgotten, and a well-liked bartender named Hersh McMillan. It also attracted more than its share of characters.

Bud Faye was one of the nicer people, quiet, unassuming, friendly. He and his mother operated a statewide chain of beauty shops.

One night my wife and I were having dinner at the Chef's Inn. Bud came wandering over from the bar to the eating section and asked if he could join us. We agreed. He called the waitress. "I wish to buy drinks for the house," he said, indicating the entire dining room.

"The whole house?"

"The whole house."

"Including the bar?"

"Of course."

About this time I got into the act. This was a Saturday night. The place was packed. It seated about 250 in the dining part, another twenty to thirty in the bar section.

"He's just kidding," I said to the waitress.

"I am not," said Bud.

"Do you realize how many drinks that is?" I asked.

Bud looked around, smiled and said, "I do." He turned to the waitress and said, "Please give everyone in the place a drink on me."

The waitress looked at me. I shrugged. "He's good for it. Go ahead."

She did.

I don't remember exactly what the drink check came to, but it was, by my standards, awesome.

Hugh Hutson was killed in an airplane accident, Claudia lost interest in the place, and from that time on the best and most popular restaurant in the whole city went through a series of managements, each equally disastrous. It was chaos. Not in order, the list as far as I can remember goes something like this:

The Chili Pepper

Alejandro's

Mario's

Barnard's

The Studio Cafe

The Corona Cafe

And now a new company has bid on the site. Only time will tell if the jinx can be broken.

ROSSI'S ITALIAN CAFE

Joe and Adelaide "Mama" Rossi ran the warmest, most delightful restaurant ever to grace Coast Highway in Corona del Mar. It was also one of the oldest restaurants, long before Tail of the Cock or the Hurley Bell. Of equal importance, they dispensed the very finest Italian food. They spoiled me. Since Rossi's, I have never found Italian food I like.

Everything was handmade, nothing from the can. Everything tasted wonderful. Once a person was exposed to Mama Rossi's meatball sandwich, no substitute would ever do.

Mama Rossi also prepared pickled mushrooms which were collector's items. Her secret? All the mushrooms were wild, picked on the hills back of town, and not a toadstool in the lot.

THE JAMAICA INN

A little later in the history of Corona del Mar, Joe Collins and Bob Ingraham built the Jamaica Inn at the corner of Avocado and Coast Highway. The food aspect was never a success, first in the hands of Fred Button who went bankrupt. Then Art LaShelle of Balboa's Christian's Hut tried his hand at it with not much better luck. Others tried, but the place never came up to the standards of other memorable restaurants on Corona del Mar's restaurant row. Despite this, the Jamaica Inn became the place to go, a worthy successor to the Chef's Inn.

And so it was that one evening I had stopped by on the way home to have a drink and talk to old friends. A man down the bar began to give me a hard time about some case I had tried. Don Vaughn, who was sitting across the bar, walked around, all six foot seven of him, dragged the guy off his bar stool, held him several feet off the ground, and shook him until I thought the guy's head was going to roll across the barroom floor. "The judge is a friend of mine," Don growled.

Once released, the man quickly apologized and made his escape.

Twenty years before, it had been Shorte Charle, all five foot six of him, who rushed to my defense. Five foot six or six foot seven, guardian angels come in all sizes, and I decided then and there that I led a charmed life in bars.

And so we move on to glamorous Electric Island, now known as Lido Isle.

BALBOA BA
10
LIDO
CHANNEL
VIA
LIDO
VIA DIJON
EBOLI
GENOA
ITHACA
JUCAR
KORON
LORCA
MENTONE
NICE
ORVIETO
PALERMO
QUITO
RAVENNA
VIA SAN REMO
VIA TRIESTE
VIA CENTRO
VIA FLORENCE
PIAZZA LIDO
VIA CENTRO
STRADA
CENTRO
LIDO ISLE
VIA HAVRE
PIAZZA GENOA
LIDO
VIA
A
A

LIDO ISLE

Book Four

LIDO ISLE

Nothing very interesting ever happened on Lido Isle.

And Yet...

At first blush Lido Isle would seem to be pretty blah. It has no bar. Thus, it could have no Dollar Dolly or Deefy Johnson. Neither was it the home base for anything as colorful as the Balboa Island Punting and Sculling Society. While Balboa had wide-open gambling, the only thing wide open about Lido Isle was the sand between vacant lots until Pappy Palmer took over. It obviously could boast of no horse stables and thus no little girls to ride bareback in the Costa Mesa Fish Fry Parade. And, as far as I know, it had no Bob Yardley to build bonfires on the bridge, thus cutting off communication between the island and the rest of the world. At least Bob has always been credited with doing that on Balboa Island, and knowing Bob, I would be the last person to question that rumor.

However, Lido Isle has, if anything, an even more peculiar history than Newport, Balboa, Balboa Island and Corona del Mar. As previously mentioned, W. S. Collins gave a mud flat known as Electric Island (or Pacific Electric Island, depending on which history you read) to Henry Huntington as part of the consideration for bringing the Pacific Electric to Newport Beach. Someplace along the way someone dredged up a lot of sand and made it into Lido Isle. Then someone got the idea of putting in a complete set of streets and hired the Griffith Company to put them in. When the lots didn't sell, the Griffith Company had to take over the island, hired P. A. (Pappy) Palmer as sales agent, and the thing took off.

That, in a nutshell, is the history of Lido Isle.

However, partway through that exhaustive history I made my first contact with Lido Isle.

Before Palmer came to the rescue of the place someone else built a scattering of houses on the island. It was during that period I had my contact.

It must have been 1928 or 1929 that Bob Blair and I secured a contract to wash the windows of those few houses as they were completed. We both lived in Balboa. Every day we would walk from Balboa to a place across the channel from Lido Isle. We would swim across, pushing our buckets, which contained our razor blades, rags and brushes, in front of us. Swimming across the narrow channel between the Balboa peninsula and the mud flat wasn't all that big a deal, but walking across that mud flat was a rite of manhood. You never saw so many stingrays, or stingarees, as we called them. We didn't dare lift our feet, or we would step on a ray, so we just shuffled along, scaring them away and cutting our feet on razor clam shells in the process. So much for the drawbacks of completing a contract to wash those damned windows–at a dollar a house. Since there weren't that many houses, our contract ran out quite early.

Bob and I still had our window-washing equipment, so we came up with a brilliant idea. The new Rendezvous had oodles of windows. We went to R. G. Burlingame, the president of the Balboa Beach Amusement Company that owned the Rendezvous, and told him we would wash all the windows in the Rendezvous for ten dollars. Unfortunately, neither Bob nor I had ever lived on the oceanfront. We didn't know that houses on the oceanfront at sea level always have gummy windows from ocean spray blown across the sand from the surf. We spent the rest of the summer washing those windows. As soon as we finished, the next day they would be gummy again. Mr. Burlingame wouldn't let us off the hook. He said it was a good lesson for us to always investigate thoroughly before going into a business venture. So much for my introduction to Lido Isle.

But back to Pappy Palmer. Through superlative selling practices he pulled Lido from a stagnant stretch of lonesome streets into the beautiful Lido Isle we all now know. It wasn't easy. A lesser man would have quit. Not Pappy. No quitter he.

Pappy also formed the Newport Balboa Federal Savings and Loan Association, and again his gutsy lending practices made it a howling success for its investors.

Pappy was one of the most charming, delightful men I have ever known. A loyal friend, a devoted family man, a super salesman, Paul Palmer is one of the great names in the history of the City of Newport Beach.

He also loved to tell stories of his meager beginnings. One day he asked me to join him and an old friend for lunch at the Arches. There I heard the story of Paul's jockey.

It seemed that this old friend and Paul were roommates during their struggling younger days. They were as poor as the proverbial church mice, but they had big ideas. Fortunately, they were the same size, so they bought one tuxedo between them. Then they saved their money, and once a month one of them would don the tuxedo and go out and mix with the wealthy people they were trying to impress.

And so the old friend said that after one of Paul's nights out on the town, he, the friend, was awakened the next morning by a knock on the door of their apartment. He opened the door but could see no one. Then a voice from down toward the floor said, "Is this Mr. Palmer's apartment?"

Paul's friend looked down, and there was a very small man. He said to the small man, "And who might you be?"

The small man replied, "I'm Mr. Palmer's jockey. He hired me last night."

It seems Paul had gotten a little carried away in trying to impress the wealthy group he had infiltrated.

Paul's friend had to break the sad news to the jockey that not only did Mr. Palmer not have a stable of horses for him to ride, he didn't have a single horse. Or a saddle, for that matter.

Another great person in the history of Newport Beach who came from Lido Isle was Dora Hill. She probably did more to bring Newport Beach into the modern era of clean, efficient government than any other single person.

Dora Hill was beautiful, with white hair, black eyebrows, classic features, and a mind like a steel trap. She was gracious, dignified, reserved–and tough as nails.

When she was elected mayor in 1954, Newport Beach was just coming out of its honky-tonk era and emerging as a year-round residential area. World War II had broken the back of the Depression. Prohibition had been repealed and the bootleggers were gone, so too wide-open gambling. Men of the stature of Braden Finch, Clyan Hall and Earl Stanley had started the town on its new road away from the honky-tonk beach resort era.

But a lot of the old town remained. Slot machines still existed, and the old gambling group still had an unhealthy influence in City Hall. A horse-and-buggy political climate still existed, and cronyism was still very much a way of life.

The first thing Mayor Hill did was to call for a realignment of the political situation. With the help of a young progressive Presbyterian minister named Jim Stewart, she put through the election of a Board of Freeholders who, under the leadership of Les Steffensen, created a new city charter which provided for the election of council members from various parts of the city.

No longer could a small group from Balboa or Newport run the town. The old guard changed. Bob Shelton became city manager. Karl Lynn Davis became city attorney. Jim Glavis became chief of police. The days of the good old boys were over.

Those of us who reside in a squeaky clean, modern progressive place to live and rear our children owe a lot to Dora Hill. Years later, I attempted to express my gratitude when I appointed her the first woman foreman of an Orange County Grand Jury.

Thus, Lido Isle can boast of having given to the City of Newport Beach two people who, in any pantheon of community heroes or heroines, would rate places of honor.

Underwood Harry C (LA) 118 Sapphire av Balboa Island
Underwood Milan (Laurel) r 120 Coral av Balboa Island
Union Oil Marine Dock Ferry Landing Balboa Island
United States Post Office Balboa (Alfonse M Hamann
    Postmaster) 307 Main st Balboa
United States Post Office Balboa Island (Mary Evalyn
    Rider Postmaster) Park av nr Marine Bal Isl
United States Post Office Corona del Mar (Florence An-
    derson Postmaster) 600 State Hiway C D M
United States Post Office Newport Beach (Wm H Adams
    Postmaster) 114 McFadden pl Newport
Unruh F W (Venice) 213 Canal st Newport
Upright Dorothy Mrs (LA) 411 E Central av Balboa
Upson John L (Dareen) slsmn Theo Robins r 124 Edge-
    water Balboa
Utman Geo E Mrs (Etiwanda) 623 W Central av Balboa

— V —

Vale Jasper (Mercedes) r 712 Poppy av Corona del Mar
Vallely Frank r 620 W Central av Balboa
VALLELY ROLAND F Boat Rentals h 620 W Central Npt
Van de Kamp's Holland Dutch Bakers 713 E Central Bal
Van Deren Mary Mrs h 1722 Miramar dr Balboa
Van Deusen Paul (LA) 121 N Bay Fr Balboa Island
Van De Verg M E Mrs (LA) 202 Amethyst av Balboa Isl
Van de Water C F Mrs (Long Bch) 3715 Coast blvd Npt
Van Dyke Stanley C (Pasa) 122 Crystal av Balboa Island
Van Landinghan C E Mrs (San Marino) 326 Lindo Balboa
Van Loon's Bakery 2112 Ocean Fr Newport
Van Patten F D Mrs (Pasadena) 21 Bay Island
Van Pelt Edwd fshmn r Balboa Pavilion
Van Pelt Geo H mechanic r Balboa Pavilion
Van Pelt Roger (LA) 906 E Central av Balboa
Van Trees Wm H r 1311 E Central av Balboa
Varian A S Mrs (LA) 502 E Surf Balboa
VARNER C K Lathing & Plastering ofc Boomer Build-
    ing Newport—733, r 123½-A 29th st Newport
Varum F R (LA) 319 Diamond av Balboa Island

And In Conclusion

The town grew, and the population moved from the original five villages to areas with such names as Beacon Bay, Harbor Island, Bay Shores, Cliffhaven, Shorecliffs, Balboa Coves, Irvine Terrace, Big Canyon, Harbor View, Eastbluff, Spyglass Hill, Dover Shores, Harbor Ridge, Westcliff—the list gets longer than the list of failed restaurants on the site of the old Chef's Inn. Nevertheless, the heart and soul, the flavor of the town, remains in the original five villages. From Deefy Johnson to Joe Beek, from Dollar Dolly to Izzy Pease, from sliding on mud flats to riding bareback in the Fish Fry parade, from Duke Kahanamoku to Shorte Charle, from blind mullet to the Tail of the Cock, this has been a little bit of history of those villages.

Nancy Gardner

And how accurate is this history? Well, some of it I lived through, so I can attest to that part. However, often at family get-togethers, my father will launch into a story about the town's fabled past. It is invariably about an event in which not only was he present but just happened to play a central role. Coincidentally, it is set far enough in the past that nobody present can possibly

167

contradict him. When he is through with his tale, while his appreciative audience is sighing its approval, a rustle is heard, a stirring, and my mother pins him with a stern glance. "Bob Gardner, we have been married over fifty years, and I have never heard that story before." Is she insinuating something? Well, that I leave to you, but I will note one of my father's favorite sayings: "Never let the truth stand in the way of a good story."

Pulley C R Mrs ofc nurse Dr Grundy r 902 W Central Npt
Purdue Ted r 405 E Central av apt 3 Balboa
Putnam Harry D (La Verne) 301 Ruby av Balboa Island
Pyle Clair C (Pasadena) 315 Marine av Balboa Island

— Q —

Quinn Ellen C h 300 35th st Newport
Quintrell Saml (Bertha N) r 114 28th st Newport

— R —

Raab Carl (Winifred T) h 911 E Central av Balboa
Rabbitt M L (LA) 310 Buena Vista blvd Balboa
Rabnett Jas A (Mary E) gdnr h 279 Laskspur C D M
Racker & Ponting (Walter Racker—Theo Ponting) fish-
    ing tackle 100 McF'adden pl Newport—251
Racker Walter (Ora Jean) tackle store h 465 San Bernar-
    dino av Newport Heights—294
Radio Shop (R H Knighten) 2209 Coast blvd Nwpt—1124
Ragan E V (Pasadena) 222 Agate av Balboa Island
Rahlman Mary K Miss nurse h 107 23rd st Newport
Railway Express Agency (E E Fitzpatrick agt) 25th st &
    Coast blvd Newport—4
Rainbolt Ira H (Ruth) rnchr h 108 Garnet av Balboa Isl
Raine Clyde E (Myrtelle) retired USN r 116 37th st Npt
Rains L P (Margaret) oilwkr r 107 31st st Newport
Ralphs Walter W (LA) 1314 W Bay av Newport
Rambo Arthur (Jean) Pacific Boat Co r 719 W Central av
    apt 1 Balboa
Rambo C J (Pacific Boat Co ofc 21st & Bay Fr Npt—287
Ramona Apts (Mrs Anna Benning mgr) 705 E Central Bal
Ramsey J H "Doc" (Mildred) mech r 3104½ Ocean Newpt
Ramsey Robt W (Ethel R) restr r 719 W Central Balboa

About The Author

Nora Lehman

Judge Robert Gardener, known not just for his for pragmatic dispensing of justice, his daily body surfing and skin diving, as well as for his witty and amusing articles for national magazines and local newspapers, was never a fan of longevity. He was quoted in a 1988 interview with the *Los Angeles Times* that "If you want to live a long time, it' s very simple. All you have to do is pick your ancestors carefully. All four of my grandparents and my parents lived into their '90s. I can' t think of anything worse." He died in his sleep in his Corona del Mar home on August 26, 2005. He was 93.

Born on December 27, 1911 in Arlington, Washington, Gardner first arrived in Newport Beach as a baby, but then was taken by his mother and railroader father to live in Green River, Wyoming for the next few years. It was during a violent railroad strike in 1921 that he was sent to live with relatives in Balboa. He was never to leave.

He thought he wanted to be a Forest Ranger, but he acquiesced to his mother's wish for him to take up law as a profession and entered the University of Southern California, where he earned both his bachelor and law degrees.

He returned to the beach area after graduation and in 1936 went into private practice doing so well on his first case - getting a hung jury for a murder suspect he was defending - that the Orange County District Attorney asked him to join the staff. Two years later he was appointed to the part-time Newport Beach Municipal Court and remained there until he joined the Navy in 1941. Rising to the rank of Lieutenant Commander he served four years on Admiral Chester Nimitz's staff in the Pacific theater.

Governor Earl Warren appointed him to the Orange County Superior Court in 1947 where he became the county's fourth judge of that rank and at the age of 36, the youngest Judge of the Superior Court in the State of California. Governor Ronald Reagan elevated him to the District Court of Appeal in 1969. Before stepping down eleven years later, he helped create a branch of the court in Santa Ana.

A moderate Republican, he often found himself at odds with conservatives in the county, and especially with R.C. Hoiles, the owner and publisher of the then *Santa Ana Register*. Gardner laughingly noted that whenever a four-judge photograph was published in the paper, no matter where he stood in the foursome, he was cropped out.

As another example of distressing some of the more conservative members of the community, he appointed a Japanese American as Foreman of the County Grand Jury. "I wanted to strike a blow for fairness," he said. The act was in response to his assignment as a naval intelligence officer to monitor the county's eighteen Japanese American farmers in 1941. When the United States was drawn into World War II and the farmers were interned, he was so disgusted he requested a transfer overseas.

Witty, amusing, but eminently pragmatic, he was dubbed *No Way Gard-*

ner by some attorneys for cutting off tortured legal arguments with a curt "No Way." When he was on the Appeals Court he'd sometimes have to make a ruling on a lower court's decision. In 1972, when the question of whether *Deep Throat*, an early pornographic film, should be allowed to continue to be shown in a local theater, a lower court judge ruled, despite the constitutionality of the question, that it was both offensive and obscene and should be banished from the theater. Shaking his head upon reading of that lower court decision, Gardner knew the case would be before him in the morning.

His pithy observations were quoted by lawyers and journalists alike.

Remarking on the so-called "no-fault" Family Law Act of 1969 he said, "The act may not be used as a handy vehicle for the summary disposal of old and used wives. A woman is not a breeding cow to be nurtured during her years of fecundity, then conveniently and economically converted to cheap steaks when past her prime."

A Juvenile Court judge for six years, Gardner's writings produced some serious reforms. He had worked diligently for juvenile rights and through his articles and speeches he managed to help change California laws to give young people the right to confront a witness against them, to have legal council and to receive notice of proceedings. Gardner was extremely proud when Supreme Court Judge Abe Fortas referred to one of his articles in making a favorable ruling giving juveniles more rights in court.

The University of Santa Clara Law Review often quoted his remarks under the heading *A Gallery of Gardner.* An example: They cited his remarks in 1973 cautioning lawyers and judges that a juror's ability to weigh all the evidence must be respected. "A juror," he said, "is not some kind of dithering nimcompoop brought in from never-never land and exposed to the harsh realities of life for the first time in a jury box."

As a Newport Beach judge, he once wrote of the time when his habit of surfing between cases was interrupted by a summons to come into court to handle an irate woman protesting a parking ticket. Not having time to stop and dress properly, he leaped behind the bench without putting his shoes or trousers on over his bathing suit. Unbeknownst to him, the front of the desk was open and when the woman saw his bare, hairy legs she paid up and fled. It being a much smaller town in those earlier days, he ran into her socially. "She explained that she thought I was naked and decided I was a flasher and might jump to my feet and expose myself."

When in 1981 he stepped down from the bench, it was not something he wanted to do. Judicial rules discouraged working past seventy, so he went job hunting. To his surprise, two years later the Department of the Interior named him Chief Justice of American Samoa. Serving there for three years he said in an interview with the *Los Angeles Times* in 1988 that "it was sort of like being king."

From 1985 until his retirement in 2000 he wrote his tales and published his second book *Bawdy Balboa* about growing up in Balboa during Prohibition. In 1993, he worked as an arbitration judge and accepted temporary appointments to the trial court.

His wife of 53 years, Katy, and a daughter Patty Gardner, preceded him in death. Another daughter, Nancy, two granddaughters and six great grandchildren survived him.

Hoagland Ray Mrs (Riverside) 1804 Ocean Fr Newport
Hoard J G Mrs h 223 Diamond av Balboa Island
HOARD—R D DR (Jeanne) Osteo ofc Balboa Inn Arcade—18, r 1580 Ocean blvd Balboa—1216
Hockaday Robt (Santa Ana) 316 Alvarado pl Balboa
Hocker B W (Sadie) Gail Apts h 305 E Bay av Balboa
Hocker Gail r 305 E Bay av Balboa
Hodgkins W W (Monrovia) 1602 Balboa av Balboa Island
HODGKINSON ROWLAND R (Florence E) chief of police h 1565 Ocean blvd Balboa
Hodkinson Leonard clk Balboa P O r 211 Agate av Bal Isl
Hoefler Philo R (Grayce) 122 Grand Canal Balboa Island
Hoefner S A Mrs sec UHSchl r 1509 Orange av Costa Mesa
Hoffman Frank (San Gabrl) 218 Pearl av Balboa Island
Hoffman Minnie Miss h 438 Tustin av Newport Heights
Hoffman Otto (Maria) painting-decorating h 106 18th Npt
Hogan Frank G (Pasa) 600 Margueriate Corona del Mar
Hogan Harley (Lenna's Cafe) r 322 Marine av Bal Isl
Hoke Audrey r 465 Santa Ana av Newport Heights
Hoke S L (Isabelle) Cafe Edgewater Balboa Tavern r 465 Santa Ana av Newport Heights
HOLBROOK H H (Dorothy) Plumbing h 3200 Coast blvd Newport—1418-W
Holcomb W K Mrs (Riverside) 1920 Court av Newport
Holcombe Dean (Mary H) h 328 El Modena av Npt Hts
Holder Mary Mrs r 109 29th st Newport
Holder T W (Htg Pk) 3411 Finley av Newport

Newport Beach Historical Society

Since 1968, the Newport Beach Historical Society has been proudly serving the distinguished communities of Balboa, Balboa Island, Corona del Mar and Newport. As a resort, the area is internationally known. A crown jewel of the Pacific Coast, Newport Beach has produced leaders of industry, technology, ecology, sport and entertainment.

The Newport Beach Historical Society has placed dozens of bronze markers to signify historic locations, past and present, throughout our area.

The Societys large photo collection grows daily.

The greatest asset of Newport history is our citizenry and their tales of adventure. The sons and daughters of Newport know how to have fun. Our Oral History Program is designed to capture and preserve these stories. We offer classes in the practice of Oral History and support our writers. We are publishers. As time passes, there is a growing urgency to this program. Volunteers are welcomed and appreciated.

The Newport Beach Historical Society is the repository for our legacy and traditions. We encourage donations of all kinds. We welcome your support and participation.

Gordy Grundy
President
2013

www.NewportBeachHistorical.com

E-mail: info@NewportBeachHistorical.com

Acknowledgments

The publishers would like to thank the following, in no particular order, for their help in the publishing of this book:

The family of Judge Robert Gardner, Nancy Gardner, Amigos Viejos, Nicki Grundy, Gay Kelly, Danny Dan, Judge J.E.T. Rutter, Bill Ficker, Senator Marian Bergeson, Corky Carroll, Jill Thrasher and Paul Wormser of the Sherman Gardens and Library, Lisa Johnson, Wills Johnson, Bill Johnson, Dr. William O. Hendricks, Charles Loos, First American Trust, Bob Dennerline, Balboa Island Museum and Historical Society, Barbara Keig, Bob Robins, Chris Jepsen, the Orange County Archive, Gina Sammis, Claude Putnam, Dr. Gordon M. and Nellie Grundy, Helen Ann Langmade, Marcia Albrecht, Tom Stillwell, members of 'I Grew Up In Newport Beach Before It Was The O.C.', Renos Gronos, Bill Finster, the City of Newport Beach, Michael Lawler and the great people of Balboa, Balboa Island, Corona del Mar and Newport Beach.

This book was designed by Gordy Grundy and printed under his supervision.

Typefaces are Garamond, designed by Claude Garamond in the 1540's. Chaillot is an ancient font without a clear history. Both were frequently used in printing and advertising when Judge Robert Gardner was running around Newport as a kid.

The cover art, also by Grundy, offers an homage to Claude George Putnam, a Southern California illustrator, ad man and cartologist. Born in 1844, Putnam was responsible for most of the elaborate maps and advertisements designed to lure the nations populace to the sweet milk and honey of California. Putman was an early member of the Newport Harbor Yacht Club. Always on deck for the stag Pirate's Cruise to Catalina, he documented the wild event in a series of famous paintings. He was a valued member of the community and founder of the Advertising Art Association of Southern California. Putnam passed away after a long productive life in 1955 at Hoag Hospital.

Made in the USA
San Bernardino, CA
10 February 2014